Ann Petry

A Bio-Bibliography

Ann Petry

A Bio-Bibliography

HAZEL ARNETT ERVIN

G.K. Hall & Co.
An Imprint of Macmillan Publishing Company
New York

Maxwell Macmillan Canada
Toronto

Maxwell Macmillan International
New York   Oxford   Singapore   Sydney

G.K. Hall & Co.
An Imprint of
Macmillan Publishing Company
866 Third Avenue
New York, NY 10022

Maxwell Macmillan Canada, Inc.
1200 Eglinton Avenue East
Suite 200
Don Mills, Ontario M3C 3N1

Macmillan Publishing Company is part of the Maxwell Communication Group
of Companies.

Library of Congress Catalog Card Number: 92-36575

Printed in the United States of America

printing number
1 2 3 4 5 6 7 8 9 10

Library of Congress Cataloging-in-Publication Data

Ervin, Hazel A.
    Ann Petry : a bio-bibliography / Hazel A. Ervin.
        p.   cm.
    Includes index.
    ISBN 0-8161-7278-1
    1. Petry, Ann, 1908 —Bibliography.   I. Title.
Z8676.9.E78   1993
[PS3531.E933]
016.813′54—dc20
                                                                92-36575
                                                                CIP

The paper used in this publication meets the minimum requirements of American
National Standard for Information Sciences—Permanence of Paper for Printed Library
Materials. ANSI Z39.48-1984.∞™

To my parents, Harrison M. and Gladys A. Arnett,
and
Professors Lettie Austin and Theodore R. Hudson

Contents

The Author

A UNCF/Mellon Fellow for 1990–91 and 1991–92 and a member of The World Who's Who of Women (Cambridge, England) and Who's Who Among Black Americans, Hazel Arnett Ervin is currently an A.B.D. candidate in African-American Literature at Howard University. She also teaches African-American Literature at Shaw University. Her dissertation is the first post–structuralist study to reveal a hidden text in Ann Petry's novels *The Street* and *Country Place*.

"With a knowledge of the name comes a distincter recognition and knowledge of the thing."

—Thoreau

"The least we owe the writer . . . is an acknowledgment of her labor."

—Barbara Christian
Black Feminist Criticism

Acknowledgments

This compiler gratefully acknowledges permission to reprint interviews from the following periodicals and books:

American Institute of the History of Pharmacy Collection, Kremers Reference Files, University of Wisconsin School of Pharmacy, for "A Visit with Ann Petry."

Artspectrum, a newsletter published by the Windham Regional Arts Council of Willimantic, Connecticut, for "An Interview with Ann Petry."

The Crisis, for James Ivey's "Ann Petry Talks about First Novel," which appeared in vol. 53, no. 2 (February 1946).

MELUS, the Journal of the Society for the Study of the Multi-Ethnic Literature of the United States, for the *MELUS* interview: "The New England Connection" by Mark K. Wilson (vol. 15, no. 2).

Reprint from *Interviews with Black Writers,* edited by John O'Brien, by permission of John O'Brien and Liveright Publishing Corporation. Copyright © 1973 by Liveright Publishing Corporation.

Chronology

1908   Ann Lane (Petry) is born October 12 in Old Saybrook, Connecticut, to Peter Clark and Bertha James Lane, the youngest of two children

1912   Enters Old Saybrook Elementary School

1922   Begins to write short stories

1925   Graduates from Old Saybrook High School

1931   Receives Ph.G. degree from Connecticut College of Pharmacy in New Haven (now School of Pharmacy at the University of Connecticut, Storrs)

Works as clerk and manager, respectively, in family drugstores in Old Saybrook and Old Lyme, Connecticut, until 1938

1938   Marries (on February 22) George D. Petry, a native of New Iberia, Louisiana

Resides at 2 East 129th Street, New York, until 1946; for a year at 2816 Bronx Park East, New York, 67, New York

Works as salesperson and as journalist for New York's *Amsterdam News* until 1941

1939   Publishes first short story, "Marie of the Cabin Club," a suspense-romance, in *Afro-American* (Baltimore) under the pen name Arnold Petri; receives a check for $5

1940   Joins the American Negro Theatre in New York. For over a year, performs as Tillie Petunia in *On Striver's Row* at the Schomburg Center for Research in Black Culture. For two years, experiences "firsthand the way in which the dialogue in a play further[s] the action."

1941   Works for New York's *People's Voice* as editor of the woman's page and as a reporter until 1944. From 1942 to 1943, writes the weekly column "The Lighter Side," a mixture of commentary and announcements on cultural, social, and political events. From the column emerge the fictitious characters Miss Jones and Miss Smith

Studies painting and drawing at New York's Harlem Art Center, concentrating on "people, landscapes . . . everything"

1942   Attends for two years Mabel Louise Robinson's workshop and course in creative writing at Columbia University; learns to critique her own and other people's works

Helps organize the Negro Women, Inc., a Harlem consumers' watch group that provides working-class women with "how-to" information for purchasing food, clothing, and furniture; holds various offices until 1947

Helps prepare skits and programs for children of laundry workers for a number of years; works out of the educational office of the Laundry Workers Joint Board

1943   Publishes in *The Crisis,* under her own name, "On Saturday the Siren Sounds at Noon." An editor at Houghton Mifflin reads the short story and inquires whether Petry is working on a novel. She suggests Petry apply for the Houghton Mifflin Literary Fellowship Award. Petry responds that she is not working on a novel but perhaps by the time the next award is offered, she might be able to submit one. The following year, the same editor at Houghton Mifflin sends Petry all the information about the Literary Fellowship and an application

Prepares newspaper releases and recruits volunteers for Harlem–Riverside Defense Council while an assistant to the secretary of the council

Prepares newspaper releases for National Association of Colored Graduate Nurses while serving as its publicity director

Joins Harlem's Play Schools Association Project at Public School No. 10 at St. Nicholas Avenue and 116th Street as recreation specialist and helps to "develop a community program for parents and children in problem areas"

1944   Competes for Houghton Mifflin's Literary Fellowship in fiction; includes in her application an outline and several chapters of *The Street*

1945   Wins Houghton Mifflin's Literary Fellowship Award in fiction; stipend is $2,400

1946   Publishes *The Street* and dedicates the novel to her mother, Bertha James Lane

Interview with James Ivey for *The Crisis*

The Best American Short Stories, 1946, edited by Martha Foley, is dedicated to Ann Petry. Included in the collection is Petry's "Like a Winding Sheet"

Placed by critics in the "School of Wright" or the "Chicago Renaissance," primarily because of certain naturalistic elements found in *The Street*

Honored by New York's Women's City Club for her "exceptional contributions to the life of New York City"

Responds to query of America's spokesperson for African-American writers, Alain Locke, about her plans for her second novel. See Alain Locke papers in the Manuscript Division of the Moorland-Spingarn Research Center at Howard University

Responds to Rosey Poole's request for biographical and bibliographical information for publications abroad. See Rosey Poole papers in the Manuscript Division of the Moorland-Spingarn Research Center at Howard University

1947 Publishes *Country Place* and dedicates the novel to her father, Peter C. Lane, and to her husband, George D. Petry

Relocates with her husband to Old Saybrook, Connecticut

Donates autographed copies of *The Street* and *Country Place* to the Countee Cullen Memorial Collection, Trevor Arnett Library, Atlanta University (now Atlanta University Center, Woodruff Library)

Agrees to turn over manuscript for *The Street* to Carl Van Vechten for inclusion in the James Weldon Johnson Memorial Collection of Negro Arts and Letters, Beinecke Rare Book and Manuscript Library, Yale University

1948 Donates letters, autographed publications (in English and in numerous translations), reviews, photographs, and the manuscript for *Country Place* to the James Weldon Johnson Memorial Collection of Negro Arts and Letters at the Beinecke Rare Book and Manuscript Library, Yale University

1949 Birth of daughter, Elisabeth Ann Petry

Death of father, Peter Clark Lane

Launches career as writer for children and young adults with *The Drugstore Cat.* The work is dedicated to Anna Houston Bush and to Anna Louise James

1953	Publishes *The Narrows* and dedicates the novel to Mabel Louise Robinson
1955	Publishes *Harriet Tubman, Conductor on the Underground Railroad* and dedicates the biography to her daughter, Elisabeth Ann
1956	Death of mother, Bertha James Lane
	The American Civil Liberties Union protests the censorship of *The Narrows* in its Censorship Bulletin and Statement on Censorship Activity
1958	Works as a writer for Columbia Pictures in Hollywood on the screenplay for Kim Novak's film *That Hill Girl*
1960	Under the auspices of the Library of Congress, *Harriet Tubman, Conductor on the Underground Railroad* is transposed into braille
1964	Publishes *Tituba of Salem Village* and dedicates the biography to her uncle Frank P. Chisholm
	Under the auspices of the Library of Congress, *Tituba of Salem Village* is recorded for the Division for the Blind
	Delivers lecture in the Central Children's Room at the New York Public Library for the Fifty-Fourth Annual Exhibition of Children's Books: "The Common Ground"
1965	Is reelected to the Board of Directors of the Author's League Fund (the Author's League of America)
1968	Donates to the "Ann Petry Collection" in Special Collections at Mugar Library, Boston University, the following: autographed publications (in English and in numerous translations), letters, "numerous" newspaper clippings of articles and reviews, manuscripts, galleys, research notes, photographs, and miscellaneous memorabilia
1970	Publishes *Legends of the Saints* and dedicates the work to her sister, Helen L. Bush
1971	Publishes *Miss Muriel and Other Stories,* the first collection of short stories by an American black woman writer, and dedicates the collection to her brother-in-law, Walter J. Petry
1972	Lectures at Miami University of Ohio
1973	Interview with John O'Brien for *Interviews with Black Writers*
	Delivers lecture on life and works at Suffolk University: "This Unforgettable Passage"
1974	Serves as visiting professor in English at the University of Hawaii
	Biography is entered in *Who's Who of American Women*

1976   Publishes first poems, "Noo York City 1," "Noo York City 2," and "Noo York City 3," in *Weid: The Sensibility Revue* (Bicentennial Issue II, American Women Poets)

1977   Biography is entered in *Who's Who Among Black Americans*

1978   Awarded creative writing grant by the National Endowment for the Arts

1981   Publishes the poems "A Purely Black Stone" and "A Real Boss Black Cat" in *A View from the Top of a Mountain*

1982   Delivers lecture at the Fourth Annual Richard Wright Lecture at Yale University

1983   Receives Doctor of Letters from Suffolk University

1984   Receives award for literature from Connecticut Historical Society, Black Women of Connecticut: Achievement Against the Odds

1985   Receives a citation for her literary achievements from the City of Philadelphia (9 April)

        The Street reprinted by Beacon Press (Black Women Writers' Series)

1986   Biography is entered in *Great Women in Connecticut History* (Hartford, CT: The Permanent Commission on the Status of Women)

        Publishes the contemporary short story "The Moses Project" (English Department, University of Massachusetts: *Harbor Review*)

1988   Interview with Mark Wilson for *MELUS*

        Receives a citation from the United Nations Association of the United States of America (28 January)

        Receives Doctor of Letters from University of Connecticut

        The Narrows and *The Drugstore Cat* reprinted by Beacon Press (Black Women Writers' Series)

1989   Interview with Hazel Arnett Ervin for *Ann Petry: A Bio-Bibliography*

        Receives the Lifetime Achievement Award (4 February) at the Fifth Annual Celebration of Black Writers' Conference at a reception held at the Friends of the Free Library in Philadelphia

        Receives Doctor of Humane Letters from Mount Holyoke College

        Biography is entered in *Who's Who in Writers, Editors and Poets*

        Miss Muriel and Other Stories reprinted by Beacon Press (Black Women Writers' Series)

1992   *The Street* reissued by Houghton Mifflin

Reveals in *American Visions* (June/July), an extensive list of personal reading preferences

Receives the Connecticut Arts Award from the Connecticut Commission on the Arts (Stamford).

Reads from her writings during the thirty-minute evening broadcast of "Connecticut Voices" on Connecticut Public Radio in Hartford. She is the first of thirteen widely known Connecticut writers invited to participate in this thirteen-week project sponsored jointly by The Connecticut Center for the Book and *Northeast* magazine in Hartford (November 14)

Attends a "Tribute to Ann Petry," with Gloria Naylor as guest speaker, at Trinity College. Prior to the tribute an Ann Petry Conference is held at which scholars from numerous colleges and universities make presentations and hold discussions

1993   Donates autographed copies of all works to the Ann Petry Collection in the African-American Research Center at Shaw University. Included in the collection are hundreds of difficult-to-find reviews and articles

Introduction

In 1939, Ann Petry received $5.00 from the *Afro-American*, a newspaper in Baltimore, Maryland, for the short story "Marie of the Cabin Club." This suspense–romance, published under the pseudonym Arnold Petri, with its multitude of coincidences surrounding espionage, kidnapping, attempted murder, and finally the rescue of a female in distress, was, according to Ann Petry, the "first" in her long writing career.[1] Four years later, in *The Crisis*, under her real name, Petry published the first of more than fifteen realistic short stories—"On Saturday the Siren Sounds." On reading this somewhat probing story about a father who loses his favorite child in a house fire, murders his wife because she neglected the child, and then takes his own life, an editor from Houghton Mifflin approached Mrs. Petry about applying for Houghton's Literary Fellowship Award in fiction. The following year, Petry made application and won a stipend of $2,400. In February of 1946, Houghton Mifflin published *The Street*. The novel soared to best-seller status, and Ann Petry became an instant success.

For more than fifty years, success for Petry has been continuous. She has published in every genre, and because of her literary presence and contributions, she has earned widespread notice, both in the United States and abroad. Such acknowledgments, appearing in book reviews, short and full-length critical studies, biographical essays, and select bibliographies, have been brought together in this compilation.[2]

Critic Barbara Christian once said, "The least we owe the writer . . . is an acknowledgment of her labor."[3] Since 1946, critics have been acknowledging the labor of Ann Petry. Although the majority of Petry's criticism has been sociological and formalist (and often superfluous in both approaches), there are palpable distinctions within her bibliography. In the 1950s, two full-length critical studies of black novelists, Carl Milton Hughes's *The Negro Novelist: 1940–1950, a Discussion of the Writings of American Negro Novelists 1940–1950* and Robert Bone's *The Negro Novel in America*, set the patterns of critical approaches to Petry, and those were sociological and formalist. Because of Hughes's and Bone's book-length critiques, which were often quoted and excerpted well into the 1970s, critics focused on Petry's indictment of a racist society in *The Street* and insisted she was a naturalist or a disciple (often a less-than-adequate disciple) of Richard Wright. Furthermore, in analyzing her raceless *Country Place,* critics insisted Petry was an assimilationist.

Many, however, whose less-known critiques appeared between 1946 and the late 1950s in newspapers and popular magazines, move the criticism of Petry's work beyond the realms of naturalism and the Wright School. For example, in the 1940s one critic in the *Pittsburgh Courier* addresses Petry as Harlem's "adopted daughter."[4] To another critic, who focuses on her style, she is an "unblushing realist,"[5] while for a third, she is an artist who approaches her characters with the "penetration of a psychiatrist . . . [and the] delicate care of a mother."[6] In *The New York Times Book Review,* reviewer Alfred Butterfield looks at the actions of Lutie Johnson in *The Street* and encourages further examinations of the narrative as Lutie's "personal epic."[7] In the *Birmingham News,* writer Mary Ellen Crane introduces thoughts on Lutie's "free will."[8] In the *Boston Chronicle,* writer William Harrison suggests comparing the action in *The Street* with the action of Greek tragedies by Sophocles and Euripides,[9] while in *New Masses,* Jose Yglesias questions whether *Country Place* is a "morality tale."[10]

In the 1950s, critics continue to approach Petry outside of any naturalistic or protest tradition. For instance, in *The Nation,* Diana Trilling explores "class" in *The Street* and encourages additional criticism—perhaps Marxist criticism—on how in the novel "class feelings . . . [are] ingrained in the black community."[11] In *The New York Times Book Review,* Wright Morris encourages a comparison of Petry's Mamie Powther in *The Narrows* with James Joyce's Molly Bloom in *Ulysses,*[12] while in the *Hartford Courant,* Sidney Clark sees similarities between Faulkner's Lena Groves in *Light in August* and Abbie Crunch in *The Narrows.* Clark also suggests the Pulitzer Prize for Petry's love story in the same novel. The critics who confine Petry to naturalistic and protest traditions as well as those who move criticism of her work beyond naturalism and protest are many, literally hundreds; in this compilation, their acknowledgments have been brought together to provide a more definitive account of Ann Petry's criticism.

Those critics writing about Petry in the very late 1960s and throughout the 1970s appear oblivious to the critiques that had appeared in newspapers and popular magazines in the 1940s and 1950s; nonetheless, they call for closer readings or reevaluations of Petry's novels. In "Perhaps Not So Soon One Morning," for example, Addison Gayle, Jr., refutes Herbert Hill's conclusion in *Soon One Morning* that James Baldwin and Ralph Ellison are the only capable forerunners of black writers entering the mainstream of American literature. To further disprove Hill, Gayle suggests that Baldwin's Ida Scott has been drawn more artistically by Petry in *The Street.*[13] Although Vernon E. Lattin in "Ann Petry and the American Dream" and David Littlejohn in *Black on White: A Critical Survey of Writing by American Negroes* are reluctant to dismiss all naturalistic or protest tendencies in Petry's novels, Lattin does insist that readers "look at [Petry's] novels freshly and . . . reevaluate." Then he shows how Petry undermines cultural notions that in America with a little effort anyone can make it.[14] David Littlejohn notes Petry's sympathetic identification in her character sketches,[15] and women critics such as Mary Helen Washington in "Black Women Image Makers"[16] and

Barbara Smith in "Toward a Black Feminist Criticism"[17] go a step further to claim Petry as a forerunner of the black women writers' literary tradition.

By the 1980s and early 1990s, critics spoke in persistent and concordant voices, insisting that Petry's criticism be moved beyond naturalistic visions and the Wright School. In an article on Petry for the *Nethula Journal*, Joyce Ann Joyce clarifies the manner in which critics are to move Petry's criticism beyond sociological approaches. She urges critics to trust Petry's donnée—her given subject or idea. Other calls come from, for example, Margaret B. McDowell in " 'The Narrows': A Fuller View of Ann Petry,"[19] Bernard Bell in "Ann Petry's Demythologizing of American Culture and Afro-American Character" and "The Triumph of Naturalism,"[20] Thulani Davis in "Family Plots: Black Women Writers Reclaim their Past,"[21] Trudier Harris in "On Southern and Northern Maids: Geography, Mammies, and Militants,"[22] Thelma Shinn in "The Women in Ann Petry's Novels,"[23] Joyce Hope Scott in "Commercial Deportation as Rite of Passage in Black Women's Novels,"[24] and by numerous other Petry critics in the forthcoming special issue of *Callaloo* in 1994 (guest editor, Lindon Barrett). There are other critics who choose to focus on Petry's responses to particular themes. For instance, Sybille Kamme-Erkel looks at "marriage" in *The Street*.[25] Nellie McKay in the Introduction to the reprint of *The Narrows* by the Black Women Writers' Series at Beacon Press and Hazel Arnett Ervin in her dissertation, "The Subversion of Cultural Ideology in Ann Petry's *The Street* and *Country Place*," direct the reader's attention to Petry's interest in patriarchal ideology and the black feminine consciousness during the 1940s and 1950s.[26] For Marjorie Pryse in her essay " 'Patterns against the Sky': Deism and Motherhood in Ann Petry's *The Street*," another theme is "motherhood."[27] In *But Some of Us Are Brave*, the editors include syllabi by leading professional black women writers/critics that offer thematic approaches to Petry's fiction.[28] From the 1970s to the present, the majority of the critiques qualify as reevaluations or close readings of Petry's donnée. Critical approaches span from rhetorical to genre to feminist and are represented in this compilation.

Not all criticism on Ann Petry has been favorable. For example, in "Mrs. Petry's Harlem," James Ivey criticizes her failure in *The Street* to depict "normal and responsible people in the [African-American] community." Ivey insists that Lutie fails because of her naivete and because of her poor choice of male friends—not because of Petry's "street."[29] In articles appearing in *The Christian Science Monitor*[30] and *Catholic World*,[31] unidentified writers question why Petry as an African-American would give such a "deplorable" impression of Harlem life. The unidentified reviewer in *Catholic World* also predicts that the sex and violence in the novel will be objectionable to some African-Americans.[32] As for Petry's *Country Place*, her early critics suggest that the novel's style is contrived and melodramatic, or that the work simply is not another *The Street*. With *The Narrows*, much unfavorable criticism concerns the novel's interracial lovers—Link, a black man, and Camilo, a white woman. Critic Charles Nichols found Petry's overall effect or style "disappointing." Over the years, with the reprints of *The Street* and *The Narrows*, which began in the mid-1980s, critical objections have followed. For instance, in the 1987 essay "'Infidelity Becomes Her': The Ambivalent Woman in the Fiction of Ann Petry," critic Mary Helen Washington, from a feminist perspective, faults Petry's "insistence on environmental determinism as an explanation for her characters' dead-end lives." Furthermore, Washington objects to Petry's ignoring such realities as women's "relationships with their families" or women's "own suppressed creativity."[34] Writer Sherley Anne Williams never really states any objections in her review of the reprint of *The Street*; yet, after efforts by previous Petry critics to move the writer beyond the shadows of Richard Wright, Chester Himes, Theodore Dreiser, or James Farrell, Williams appears to return Petry's criticism to such prescribed notions at mid-century when she writes that the novel earns Petry "an abiding place among American naturalist novelists."[35]

In this compilation, there are 398 secondary entries. Only those that I could examine have been included.[36] The sources that are included, however, signal immense interest by critics in Ann Petry—yesterday, today, and tomorrow.

If one were to ask Mrs. Petry for which of all her works she would want to be remembered, her response would be, "I want to be remembered for everything I've written."[37] She once remarked, "I try to write so that what I've written will be remembered, whether it's a character or a situation or believable dialogue that will leave a lasting impression."[38] At present, her work consists of three novels, sixteen short stories, five poems, one children's book, three juvenile works, and collectively, more than twenty-five book reviews and articles. The most reviewed work by Ann Petry is *The Street*. The children's work, *The Drugstore Cat,* the juvenile work *The Legends of the Saints,* and Petry's five poems are the least reviewed.

In this compilation, all of Petry's works are recognized as well as the majority of her criticism. In addition, critiques have been arranged in the Index according to their focus on characterization, style, and structure, particularly for Petry's three novels, the collection of short stories *Miss Muriel and Other Stories,* and the juvenile works *Harriet Tubman, Conductor on the Underground Railroad* and *Tituba of Salem Village.* Furthermore, primary works have been cross-referenced to emphasize reprints and translations. Secondary works have also been cross-referenced.

The title of this compilation promises as well a biographical account of Ann Petry's life. No one portion of the book, however, is devoted specifically to biography. The Chronology, which has been edited by Mrs. Petry, exists primarily to correct errors that have been perpetuated over the years, such as Petry's birthdate, her marital status, her actual publications, when she graduated from high school, and where she has lectured.[39] In the works sections, there are biographical articles as well as interviews that provide information about Petry's life. Particularly in their introductions, interviewers James Ivey and John O'Brien offer family background and character sketches of the artist. In his *MELUS* interview "Ann Petry—The New England Connection," Mark K. Wilson questions Petry about her childhood and her parents. In three additional interviews, all of which are printed or reprinted here for the first time in book form, the interviewers question Petry extensively about her life, particularly in "A Visit with Ann Petry." Although not originally planned, the Chronology attempts to frame Petry's literary development. For instance, Petry uses landscapes as titles for her novels as well as for settings in her many short stories and novels. Thus, as if to draw a correlation, the Chronology indicates that shortly after the would-be artist arrives in New York City in 1938, she studies painting, concentrating on "people, landscapes . . . everything."[40] Petry's critics generally applaud her for her swift and moving style. The Chronology includes, therefore, the fact that during her two years with the American Negro Theatre, Petry experienced "firsthand the way in which the dialogue in a play further[s] the action."[41] And, of course, there are those years that Petry studied under Mabel Louise Robinson. As the Chronology notes, under the tutelage of Robinson, Petry learned to critique her own as well as other people's works.[42] If a chronology is to offer dates and events in sequential order, then, the purpose of this Chronology is to do that and more. In the index, I attempt to do more than direct readers to subjects and authors identified in the book's annotations, that is, a number of subjects and authors do not appear in the annotations but are deemed important to the new approaches to Petry's criticism and therefore have been placed in the index.

Louis I. Bredvold once said that it is the business of the critic to emphasize not the tangential but the essential and characteristic excellence of his (or her) author.[43] For scholars, critics, educators, graduate students, and all others, I have tried my best to emphasize the essential characteristics of Ann Petry's life as well as her works (primary and secondary in English and in translations), using the best sources that I know—Mrs. Petry, her critics, and myself. I trust this compilation will be helpful, expecially to those who appreciate Ann Petry as much as I and others do.

Some offerings of appreciation are in order. First, I want to express immense gratitude to Mrs. Petry—literary mother, heroine, teacher, and friend. Then I want to thank the thoughtful librarians at the following universities: Atlanta University Center, Boston, Duke, Fisk, Howard, North Carolina Central, the University of Minnesota, and Yale. For their assistance, I am grateful to Janet Sims-Woods and others at the Moorland-Spingarn Research Center at Howard, curator Patricia Willis and others at the Beinecke Rare Book and Manuscript Library at Yale, Bettye McCullough in Archives/Special Collections at the Woodruff (Atlanta University Center), the staff both at the Schomburg Center for Research in Black Culture in New York and at the Martin Luther King, Jr., Public Library in Washington, DC. A heartfelt thank you to Charles Niles and all others in Special Collections at the Mugar Library at Boston University. Thank you to Dr. Alphonso Frost at Howard University for his English translation of German writer Sabine Brock's study of *The Street* and to Michel Fabre in Paris, France, for his prompt response to my query on Chester Himes. Of course, I wish to thank Mary Poole and Mrs. Mildred Mason, who on many occasions helped me to get in and out of my computer. Thank you, E. Ethelbert Miller, Christopher Arnett, Kevin Ervin, Antionette Kerr, Ann Shockley, Blyden Jackson, Stephen Henderson, and Jon Woodson. To the many people whom I have spoken with at conferences or over the telephone, requesting information, articles, books, and photographs of Petry for this compilation,[44] thanks for your contributions.

NOTES

1. Letter dated 12 May 1988 from Ann Petry to Hazel A. Ervin.
2. I am particularly grateful to James Lee Hill for his compilation of numerous secondary sources on Petry in *Bibliography of the Works of Chester Himes, Ann Petry, and Frank Yerby*; to Carol Fairbank and Eugene Engeldinger for their compilation of secondary works in *Black American Fiction: A Bibliography*; and to those persons who included bibliographies on Petry in their dissertations, which served to disclose other sources in Petry's bibliography.
3. Barbara Christian, *Black Feminist Criticism: Perspectives on Black Women Writers* (New York: Pergamon, 1985), xi.
4. James E. Fuller, "Harlem Portrait," *Pittsburgh Courier,* 9 February 1946 [Special Collections, Boston University].
5. Arna Bontemps, "Tough, Carnal Harlem," *New York Herald Tribune Weekly Book Review,* 10 February 1946, 4.
6. Ben Burns, "Off the Book Shelf," *Chicago Defender*, 9 February 1946 [Special Collections, Boston University].
7. Alfred Butterfield, "The Dark Heartbeat of Harlem," *New York Times Book Review,* 10 February 1946, 6.
8. Mary Ellen Crane, "Life in Harlem," *Birmingham News* 9 March 1946 [Special Collections, Boston University].
9. William Harrison, review of *The Street, Boston Chronicle,* 23 February 1946 [Special Collections, Boston University].
10. Jose Yglesias, "Classy-Type People," *New Masses,* 9 December 1947 [Special Collections, Boston University].
11. Diana Trilling, "Class and Color," *The Nation* 162 (9 March 1946): 290–291.
12. Wright Morris, "The Complexity of Evil," *New York Times Book Review,* 16 August 1953, 4.
13. Addison Gayle, Jr., "Perhaps Not So Soon One Morning," *Phylon* 26, no. 4 (Winter 1968): 397.
14. Vernon E. Lattin, "Ann Petry and the American Dream," *Black American Literature Forum* 12, no. 2 (Summer 1978): 69–72.
15. David Littlejohn, *Black on White: A Critical Survey of Writing by American Negroes* (New York: Viking, 1966).
16. Mary Helen Washington, "Black Women Image Makers," *Black World* 23, no. 10 (August 1974): 11.
17. Barbara Smith, "Toward a Black Feminist Criticism," *Conditions: Two* 1, no. 2 (October 1977): 25–42.
18. Joyce Ann Joyce, Ann Petry. *Nethula Journal* 2 (1982): 16–20. Joyce's use of the word "donnée" is defined further by that of Henry James in "The Art of Fiction."
19. Margaret B. McDowell, " 'The Narrows': A Fuller View of Ann Petry," *Black American Literature Forum* 14, no. 4 (Winter 1980): 135–141.
20. Bernard W. Bell, "Ann Petry's Demythologizing of American Culture and Afro-American Character." *Conjuring: Black Women, Fiction, and Literary Tradition,* ed. Marjorie Pryse and Hortense J. Spillers (Bloomington: Indiana University Press,

1985); "The Triumph of Naturalism," *The Afro-American Novel and Its Tradition* (Amherst: University of Massachusetts Press, 1987. Reprint. 1989).

21. Thulani Davis, "Family Plots: Black Women Writers Reclaim Their Past," *The Village Voice* 32, no. 10 (10 March 1987): 14–17.

22. Trudier Harris, "On Southern and Northern Maids: Geography, Mammies, and Militants," *From Mammies to Militants: Domestics in Black American Literature* (Philadelphia: Temple University Press, 1982).

23. Thelma J. Shinn, "Women in the Novels of Ann Petry," *Critique, Studies in Modern Fiction* 16, no. 1 (1974): 110–120.

24. Joyce Hope Scott, "Commercial Deportation as Rite of Passage in Black Women's Novels," *Matatu* 3, no. 6 (1989): 127–154.

25. Sybille Kamme-Erkel, *Happily Every After?: Marriage and Its Rejection in Afro-American Novels* (New York: Peter Lang, 1989).

26. Nellie McKay, Introduction, *The Narrows* (Boston: Beacon, 1988). See also Nellie Y. McKay, "Ann Petry's *The Street* and *The Narrows*: A Study of the Influence of Class, Race, and Gender on Afro-American Women's Lives" in *Women and War: The Changing Status of American Women from the 1930's to the 1950's,* ed. Maria Diedrich and Dorothea Fischer-Hornang (New York: Berg, 1990); Hazel Arnett Ervin, "The Subversion of Cultural Ideology in Ann Petry's *The Street* and *Country Place,*" Ph.D. diss., Howard University, 1993.

27. Marjorie Pryse, " 'Patterns against the Sky': Deism and Motherhood in Ann Petry's *The Street.*" *Conjuring: Black Women, Fiction, and Literary Tradition,* ed. Marjorie Pryse and Hortense J. Spillers (Bloomington: Indiana University Press, 1985).

28. Gloria T. Hall, Patricia Bell Scott, and Barbara Smith, eds., *All the Women Are White, All the Blacks Are Men, But Some of Us Are Brave* (Old Westbury, NY: The Feminist Press, 1982).

29. James Ivey, "Mrs. Petry's Harlem," *Crisis* 53, no. 5 (May 1946): 154–155.

30. M. W., "The Latest Negro Novel," *Christian Science Monitor,* 8 February 1946, 14.

31. Review of *The Street, Catholic World* 163 (May 1946): 187. For additional critiques that might be considered unfavorable, see Petry in the Index to this book.

32. Ibid.

33. Charles H. Nichols, "New England Narrative," *Phylon* 14, no. 4 (Fourth Quarter 1953): 437.

34. Mary Helen Washington, " 'Infidelity Becomes Her': The Ambivalent Woman in the Fiction of Ann Petry." *Invented Lives: Narratives of Black Women, 1860–1960* (Garden City, NY: Anchor/Doubleday, 1987), 298. One might add, however, that Washington's criticism simultaneously encourages further feminist readings of Petry. After all, she follows her critical comments with an excerpt from *The Narrows*—an excerpt that highlights the assertive and individualistic Mamie Powther—and she titles the excerpt simply "Mamie."

35. Sherley Anne Williams, Review of *The Street, MS* (23 September 1986), 23.

36. For example, I have excluded Chester Himes's review of *The Street*. In a letter dated 7 November 1991 from Michel Fabre, who is compiling Chester Himes's bibliography, I learned that Himes's review of *The Street,* which has been recorded by Petry's critics as "missing," was unpublished. I have been unable to examine this unpublished review; therefore, I have not included an entry for it in this compilation. Papers read at conferences have been omitted for similar reasons.

37. See Hazel Arnett Ervin, "Just a Few Questions More, Mrs. Petry" in this volume.

38. "A Visit with Ann Petry," American Institute of the History of Pharmacy Collections, Kremers Reference Files (University of Wisconsin School of Pharmacy), 19. See interview in this book.
39. Many of Petry's lectures have been omitted because I could not verify the dates and actual purposes of them.
40. Ann Petry, *Contemporary Authors: Autobiography Series,* vol. 6 (Detroit: Gale Research, 1988).
41. Ibid.
42. See "Just a Few Questions More, Mrs. Petry" in this volume.
43. Louis I. Bredvold, *The Literature of the Restoration and the Eighteenth Century, 1660–1798* (New York: Collier, 1962).
44. Ann Petry really dislikes photographs. She believes pictures take away from one's spirit and reality. To honor her request, the many pictures collected for this book were removed.

Ann Petry

A Bio-Bibliography

Primary Works

Fiction

1 "The Bones of Louella Brown." *Opportunity: Negro Journal of Life* 25, no. 4 (October–December 1947): 189–192, 226–230. Also appears in *Miss Muriel and Other Stories,* by Ann Petry. Boston: Houghton Mifflin, 1971. Reprint. Boston: Beacon, 1989.

   A Harvard graduate student attempts to study the bone structure of white and black women and inadvertently mixes up the "astonishingly" identical remains of two of them: the Countess of Castro, a white woman, and Louella Brown, a black woman and laundress to the Countess. Which of them will be buried in Boston's all-white Bedford Abbey Cemetery? This becomes the perplexing question for several Bostonian conservatives—that is, until the ghost of Louella Brown returns.

2 *Country Place.* Boston: Houghton Mifflin, 1947. Reprint. London: Michael Joseph, Ltd., 1948. Reprint. Chatham, NJ: Chatham Bookseller, 1971. Foreign Reprint *Tempeste.* Translated by V. E. Bravetta. Roma: Jandi Sapi, 1949.

   Like the powerful thunderstorms that disrupt the pastoral town of Lennox, several characters are uncontrollable and disruptive when their lives intertwine with the lives of others in that New England setting.

3 "Doby's Gone." *Phylon* 5, no. 4 (Fourth Quarter 1944): 361–66. Also appears in *Miss Muriel and Other Stories,* by Ann Petry. Boston: Houghton Mifflin. 1971. Reprint. Boston: Beacon, 1989. *The Third Woman.* Edited by Dexter Fisher. Boston: Houghton Mifflin, 1980.

   A close relationship between six-year-old Sue Johnson and her imaginary friend Doby comes to an end when Sue enters the first grade.

4 "Has Anybody Seen Miss Dora Dean?" *New Yorker* (October–November 1958): 41–48. Also appears in *Miss Muriel and Other Stories,* by Ann Petry. Boston: Houghton Mifflin, 1971. Reprint. Boston: Beacon, 1989.

   A young and nameless female narrator is summoned to the home of Sarah Forbes—an old friend of the narrator's parents—to honor Sarah's death wish. The story is told as the narrator, en route to the Forbes's home, recollects the circumstances surrounding Sarah's death—her marriage to Peter Forbes and, three weeks later, their living in separate quarters because Forbes had to return to his live-in employment with Mrs. Wingate. Then, there are Forbes's promiscuous activities with beautiful girls in Shacktown, followed by his suicide. The title of the short story is a tune made famous by Bert Williams and George Walker during the twenties, suggesting "cake-walks, beautiful brown girls, and ragtimes." The tune becomes a leitmotif for Peter Forbes throughout the story.

5 "In Darkness and Confusion." In *Cross Section*. Edited by Edwin Seaver. New York: L. B. Fisher, 1947, 98–128. Also appears in *Black Voices*. Edited by Abraham Chapman. New York: New American Library, 1968. Reprint, 1978. *Right On: An Anthology of Black Literature*. Edited by Bradford Chambers and Rebecca Moon. New York: New American Library, 1970. *Harlem*. Edited by John Henrik Clarke. New York: New American Library, 1970. *Miss Muriel and Other Stories,* by Ann Petry. Boston: Houghton Mifflin, 1971. Reprint. Boston: Beacon, 1989. Foreign Reprint. *Harlem Story*. Edited by Giichi Ouchi and Mikio Suzuki. Tokyo: Kaibunsha Ltd., n.d.

   The story involves psychological probings, particularly into the minds of three oppressed characters who purge themselves of built-up frustrations and anger when they participate in a riot that becomes ritualistic.

6 "Like a Winding Sheet." *Crisis* 52, no. 11 (November 1945): 317–318, 331–332. Also appears in *Best American Short Stories*. Edited by Martha Foley. Boston: Houghton Mifflin, 1946. *From the Roots: Short Stories by Black Americans*. Edited by Charles L. James. New York: Dodd, Mead, 1970. *Black Literature in America*. Edited by Houston A. Baker. New York: McGraw-Hill, 1971. *Miss Muriel and Other Stories,* by Ann Petry. Boston: Houghton Mifflin, 1971. Reprint. Boston: Beacon, 1989. *Black Writers of America: A Comprehensive Anthology*. Edited by Richard Barksdale and Keneth Kinnamon. New York: Macmillan, 1972. *New Cavalcade: African-American Writing from 1760 to Present*. Edited by Arthur P. Davis, J. Saunders Redding, and Joyce Ann Joyce. Vol. 1. Washington, DC: Howard University Press, 1991.

   With continuous references to his hands, Petry introduces main character Mr. Johnson, and foreshadows for him a violent outcome: after a racially motivated incident, the stressed and discontented Mr. Johnson loses his self-control, and, with his hands, murders the one person who has been his longtime companion throughout the story—his wife.

7 "Marie of the Cabin Club." *Afro-American* (Baltimore), 19 August 1939, 14.
   This suspense–romance, written under the pseudonym Arnold Petri, is Petry's first publication in short fiction. Marie, a cigarette girl at the Cabin

Club, is kidnapped by a villainous English spy and used to entrap her friend Georgie Barr, a musician at the jazz club and a spy for France. When Barr refuses to turn over secret intelligence to the Englishman, he and Marie are told they will die. The New York police, however, intervene. Once out of danger, Georgie confesses his love for Marie and asks her to marry him.

8 "The Migraine Workers." *Redbook* (May 1967): 66–67, 125–127. Also appears in *Miss Muriel and Other Stories,* by Ann Petry. Boston: Houghton Mifflin, 1971. Reprint. Boston: Beacon, 1989. *Feminine Fiction from Across America.* Edited by Tettuo Yamaguchi and Midori Sasaki. Tokyo: Bunri Co., Ltd., n.d.

   The owner of a service station feeds a poor and undernourished migrant worker who escapes his migratory job in order to survive. Before the story ends, the simple act of turning the migrant worker over to his employer becomes a painful decision for the service station owner.

9 "Miss Muriel." In *Soon One Morning: New Writing by American Negroes, 1940–1962.* Edited by Herbert Hill. New York: Knopf, 1963, 166–209. Reprint. 1965. Also appears in *Stories in Black and White.* Edited by Eva Kissin. Philadelphia: Lippincott, 1970. *Miss Muriel and Other Stories,* by Ann Petry. Boston: Houghton Mifflin, 1971. Reprint. Boston: Beacon, 1989.

   A nameless child who has lived a protected and carefree life in a small New England town loses this state of innocence when she takes a stand against her uncle and his friend, who deliberately run out of town her friend Mr. Bemish—a white man—because Mr. Bemish wants to marry her Aunt Sophronia—a black woman.

10 "The Moses Project." *Harbor Review* (English Department, University of Massachusetts), no. 5/6 (1986): 52–61.

   Contemporary trickster Joe Cooper is sentenced to weekend house arrest for neglecting to pay $300 in fines for traffic tickets. A transmitter attached to Cooper's leg monitors his movements and beeps whenever he goes outside his confined space. Cooper, however, is a skilled mechanic and an expert locksmith. He outwits the authorities and spends his weekends away from home.

11 "Mother Africa." *Miss Muriel and Other Stories,* by Ann Petry. Boston: Houghton Mifflin, 1971. Reprint. Boston: Beacon, 1989.

   The main character, Mannie, an Everyman, idolizes a female statue that he calls the sable Mother Africa. The statue, however, is really an "alive-looking [white female] statue," used by the omniscient narrator to satirize the colonization of the African-American mind.

12 *The Narrows.* Boston: Houghton Mifflin, 1953. Reprint. London: Gollancz, 1954. Reprint. New York: Signet, 1955. Reprint. London: Ace Books Lim-

ited, 1961. Reprint. New York: Pyramid, 1971. Reprint. Boston: Beacon, 1988. Also appears as excerpt, "Mamie," in *Invented Lives: Narratives of Black Women 1860–1960.* Edited by Mary Helen Washington. Garden City, NY: Anchor/Doubleday, 1987. Foreign Reprint. *Link und Camilo.* Berlin: Propylaen-Verlag, 1955.

A black man and a white woman are in love. Yet for reasons extending as far back as slavery, such an affair is taboo, even in New England.

13 "The Necessary Knocking at the Door." *The Magazine of the Year 1947* (August 1947): 39–44. Also appears in *Miss Muriel and Other Stories,* by Ann Petry. Boston: Houghton Mifflin, 1971. Reprint. Boston: Beacon, 1989. *Strange Barriers.* Edited by J. Vernon Shea. New York: Lion Library Editions, 1955.

Early in the day at a religious convention, the southern conservative Mrs. Gib Taylor hurls a two-syllable hate word at main character Alice. Late in the night, Alice overhears Mrs. Taylor moaning as if she were seriously ill. But after Mrs. Taylor's racial epithet earlier in the day, Alice cannot force herself to knock, to enter, and to inquire. By morning, Mrs. Taylor is dead. The story ends questioning the actions of both women.

14 "The New Mirror." *New Yorker* (29 May 1965): 28–36, 38, 40, 43–44, 46, 49–50, 52, 55. Also appears in *Miss Muriel and Other Stories,* by Ann Petry. Boston: Houghton Mifflin, 1971. Reprint. Boston: Beacon, 1989. *Out of Lines: A Selection of Contemporary Black Fiction.* Edited by Quandra Stadler. Washington, DC: Howard University Press, 1975.

The "private" lives of the Layen family—"those rare laboratory specimens [of] black people who [run] the [only] drugstore in the white town of Wheeling, New York"—are interrupted when father Layen disappears for almost a day. His wife and sister-in-law do not know that he has secretly gone to get a set of false teeth; they must decide whether to inform the police and the public that someone from their private world is missing.

15 "Olaf and His Girl Friend." *Crisis* 52, no. 5 (May 1945): 135–137, 147. Also appears in *Miss Muriel and Other Stories,* by Ann Petry. Boston: Houghton Mifflin, 1971. Reprint. Boston: Beacon, 1989.

Told from the perspective of an observant painter, this short story is about one man's courageous and successful attempt to be reunited with the woman he loves. The grandmother of Belle Rose prevents Belle from marrying the Barbadian Olaf by resetting the girl in Harlem. After crossing the ocean, however, Olaf finally finds Belle Rose and reclaims her as his only love.

16 "On Saturday the Siren Sounds at Noon." *Crisis* 50, no. 12 (December 1943): 368–369.

Minutes before the nameless protagonist commits suicide by jumping in front of a moving train, the sound of a siren and the sight of metallic train tracks evoke memories of his return home from work to find the charred and still body of his favorite child, and the terribly burned bodies of his other two children. The children had been locked inside their tiny Harlem apartment by their mother while she went out. The protagonist murders the negligent mother, and as the story comes full circle, he commits suicide. This short story is the first to appear under Petry's name.

17 "Solo on the Drums." *The Magazine of the Year 1947* (October 1947): 105–110. Also appears in *Miss Muriel and Other Stories,* by Ann Petry. Boston: Houghton Mifflin, 1971. Reprint. Boston: Beacon, 1989. *American Negro Short Stories.* Edited by John Clarke. New York: Hill and Wang, 1966.

This story, with a familiar theme of boy loses girl, shows the influence of jazz. Shortly before drummer Kid Jones's performance, he discovers that his wife plans to leave him for the piano player in his musical group. Enraged and humiliated, Jones manages to go on stage and perform. His "pulse beat . . . becomes one with the drums," and by the end of the performance (and the story), he has purged himself of his anger, pain, and humiliation.

18 *The Street.* Boston: Houghton Mifflin, 1946. Reprint. New York: Pyramid, 1946, 1961. Reprint. London: Michael Joseph, Ltd., 1947. Reprint. New York: Signet, 1947. Reprint. Boston: Beacon, 1985. Reissue. Boston: Houghton Mifflin, 1992. In condensations: *Afro-American Literature: Fiction.* Compiled by William Adams, Peter Conn, and Barry Slepian. Boston: Houghton Mifflin, 1970. *African-American Literature, Voices of a Tradition.* Chicago: Holt, Rinehart and Winston, 1992. *Cavalcade: Negro American Writing from 1760 to the Present.* Edited by Arthur P. Davis and J. Saunders Redding. Boston: Houghton Mifflin, 1971. *The Ghetto Reader.* Edited by David P. Demarest and Lois S. Lamdin. New York: Random House, 1970. *Negro Digest* 4, no. 7 (May 1946): 84–98. *Intimate Relationships: Marriage, Family and Lifestyles through Literature.* Edited by Rose M. Somerville. Englewood Cliffs, NJ: Prentice-Hall, 1975. Foreign Reprints: *A Rua.* Translated by Ligia Junqueira Smith. Sao Paulo, Brazil: Companhia Editoru Nacional, 1947. *De Straat.* Translated by Vertaald Door and H. W. J. Schaap. Amsterdam: N. Y. De Arbeiderspers, 1948. *De Stratte.* Berlin: Druck and Veratbeitung. *Die Strasse.* Translated by von Marinette Chenaud. Bern, Switzerland: Verlag Hallwag Bern, n.d. *En Kvinne I Harlem.* Translated by Oversatt Av Erik Farland. Oslo: Tiden, 1947. *Gaden.* Copenhagen: Aschenog Dansk Forlag Kobenhaun, 1946. *Gatan.* Translated by Olof Hogstadius. Stockholm: Ljus, 1947. *La Calle.* Translated by Julio Vacarezza. Argentina: Ediciones Penser, n.d. *La Rehob.* Translated by Aaron Amir. Tel-Aviv: N. Tversky Publishing House, Ltd., 1947. *La Rue.* Translated by Martine Monod, Nicole Soupault, and Philippe Soupault.

Paris: Charlot, 1948. *The Street.* Translated by Ryo Namikawa. Tokyo: Kaizo Sha, 1950. Foreign Excerpts: *L'Arche* 4, no. 23 (Janvier 1947): 47–86 (translated by Nicole and Philippe Soupault). *L'Arche* 6, no. 24 (Fevrier 1947): 42–79. *L'Arche* 7, no. 25 (Marche 1947): 61–96. *L'Arche* 8, no. 26 (Avril 1947): 71–106. *Omnibook* (March 1946): 1–40; *Omnilibro* 8 (August 1946): 113–144.

In this best-seller, Lutie Johnson is defeated in her attempts as a single parent to improve conditions for herself and her eight-year-old son. She adamantly refuses, however, to become a prostitute, the last option she has, even if it means committing a murder.

19 "That Hill Girl." Hollywood, CA: Columbia Pictures, 1958.

A script that is, according to Mrs. Petry, probably still filed away at Columbia Pictures in Hollywood.

20 "The Witness." *Redbook* (February 1971): 80–81, 126–134. Also appears [slightly revised] in *Miss Muriel and Other Stories,* by Ann Petry. Boston: Houghton Mifflin, 1971. Reprint. Boston: Beacon, 1989; *Studies in the Short Story.* Edited by Virgin Scott and David Madden. Chicago: Holt, Rinehart and Winston, 1976. *The World of Fiction.* Edited by David Madden. Chicago: Holt, Rinehart and Winston, 1990.

A group of egregious middle-class white youths and a black middle-class educator, Mr. Woodruff, commit a crime. The white youths kidnap, assault, and rape a young white female. Mr. Woodruff, who is also kidnapped by the youths and implicated in the crime when he is made a witness, sees himself only as a black man who might be accused of raping a white woman. Therefore, once released by the youths, Mr. Woodruff leaves town, abandoning the female victim to her executioners.

Children

21 *The Drugstore Cat* (illustrated by Susanne Suba). New York: Crowell, 1949. Reprint. Boston: Beacon, 1988.

Buzzie, a short-tempered cat, redeems himself when he saves his owner's drugstore from a "potential disaster."

Juvenile

22 *Harriet Tubman, Conductor on the Underground Railroad.* New York: Crowell, 1955. Reprint. New York: Washington Square, 1971. London: Methuen, 1960 (published as *The Girl Called Moses: A Story Biography of Harriet Tubman* with illustrations by Judith Valentine). Also appears in *Braille Book for Juvenile Readers.* Washington, DC: Library of Congress,

1960. Excerpt: *Projection in Literature,* America Reads Series. Chicago: Scott, Foresman, 1967. Foreign Reprint. *Het Leven van Harriet Tubman.* Translated by Geschiedenis Voor Jenge Mensen. Amsterdam: C. P. J. Van der Peet.

A poignant biography that traces the development of the woman who would lead 300 American slaves to freedom and would become known as the "Moses" of her race. Each chapter concludes with information that is factual and relevant to either Harriet Tubman's personal development or to the abolitionist cause.

23 *Legends of the Saints* (illustrations by Anne Rockwell). New York: Crowell, 1970.

This text shows that saints come in all nationalities, even African-American.

24 *Tituba of Salem Village.* New York: Crowell, 1964. Reprint. New York: Harper, 1988. Recorded. Division for the Blind. Washington, DC: Library of Congress, 1964.

According to this biography, the Salem trials for witchcraft were not restricted only to white Americans.

Poetry

25 "Noo York City 1." *Weid: The Sensibility Revue* (Bicentennial Issue II, American Women Poets) 12, nos. 45, 46, 47 (December 1976): 125.

Cockroaches "keep comin' forth" on the buses in New York City. The speaker tells why.

26 "Noo York City 2." *Weid: The Sensibility Revue* (Bicentennial Issue II, American Women Poets) 12, nos. 45, 46, 47 (December 1976): 126.

A laundryman's concerns, which are simply about survival, are captured in repetitive lines.

27 "Noo York City 3." *Weid: The Sensibility Revue* (Bicentennial Issue II, American Women Poets) 12, nos. 45, 46, 47 (December 1976): 127.

Auntie Jennifer Jones's health is critical to the speaker because "she so old/she so black."

28 "A Purely Black Stone." In *A View from the Top of the Mountain.* Edited by Tom Koontz and Thòm Tammaro. Daleville, IN: Barnwood Press Cooperative, 1981, 75.

The deceased Mr. Ed is mourned by employees at the "laun-de-ree store." On the grave of the deceased there is to be placed "a purely black stone." In form, this poem is reminiscent of New Black poetry.

29 "A Real Boss Black Cat." In *A View from the Top of the Mountain*. Edited by Tom Koontz and Thom Tammaro. Daleville, IN: Barnwood Press Cooperative, 1981, 76.

    The speaker is overheard wishing to be like the real boss black cat that "can fly." In form, this poem is reminiscent of New Black poetry.

Collection

30 *Miss Muriel and Other Stories*. Boston: Houghton Mifflin, 1971. Reprint. Boston: Beacon, 1989.

    Short stories written by Petry as early as 1943 and as late as 1971 are gathered in this first collection of short fiction by an African-American woman writer.

Autobiography

31 Ann Petry. In *Contemporary Authors: Autobiography Series,* vol. 6. Detroit: Gale Research, 1988.

    In detailed and lengthy recollections, Petry talks about living among colorful, proud, and ingenious family members; about how she developed as a writer, and about how she manages her success. She frequently calls herself a survivor and a gambler. Family photographs are also provided.

32 "My Most Humilitating Jim Crow Experience." *Negro Digest* 4, no. 8 (June 1946): 63–64.

    Petry recalls how, at age seven, while on a Sunday school picnic at a beach, she and members of her class were forced to leave because she was black.

Nonfiction

33 "Actress Says Coast Takes War in Stride." *People's Voice,* 14 February 1942, 18.

    Reporter Ann Petry takes the reader to the New York apartment of Hollywood actress Fredi Washington, better known as Peola in "Imitation of Life." Off-screen character sketches of Washington are drawn from a descriptive-narrative interview. Presented also are Washington's brief comments on how "Negro" troops and other members of her race on the West Coast are managing after Japan's attack on Pearl Harbor.

34 "Ann Petry on Roy De Carava's and Langston Hughes's 'The Sweet Flypaper of Life.'" In *Rediscoveries II.* Edited by David Madden and Peggy Bach. New York: Carroll and Graf, 1972.

A review of the 1985 reprint of Langston Hughes's *The Sweet Flypaper of Life,* which includes photographs by Roy De Carava. Petry calls attention to the disclaimer in bibliographies and in the front of *The Sweet Flypaper of Life* that this work is a novel. She concludes that Hughes has created "a believable home," and expresses her hope that the book remain forever in print.

35 "Annice Hairston Succeeded with Energy and Imagination." *People's Voice,* 18 April 1942, 18.

Reveals how Annice Hairston turns a hobby (knitting) into a thriving business in downtown New York—Hairston's Knitting Nook. Annice's regular clientele number around 500, some as far away as Florida.

36 "A Letter from Ann Petry." *Crisis* 54, no. 5 (May 1947): 156.

Petry informs the editors at *Crisis* that she has sold to the Danish the serial rights to "Like a Winding Sheet." The short story first appeared in *Crisis.*

37 "A Novel about a Writer Who Tried Being a Jew." *PM* (2 March 1947): 15–16.

A book review of Laura Z. Hobson's *Gentleman's Agreement.* Petry predicts that for some time to come, readers will squirm and argue over the evidence gathered by Hobson's gentile character who, upon pretending to be a Jew, finds anti-Semitism in the professional business world.

38 "An Open Letter to Mayor La Guardia." *People's Voice,* 22 May 1943, 4.

Seeks the mayor's assistance in reopening the Savoy Ballroom. Reminds the mayor that in the past the facility had been a place of entertainment for the black community as well as a place for civic organizations like the National Association for the Advancement of Colored People (NAACP) and the National Urban League to hold events that benefited the community.

39 "Canalboat to Freedom." *New York Times Book Review,* 14 August 1966, 24.

A brief review of Thomas Fall's *Canalboat to Freedom,* a historical novel that is said to show "clearly" the working of the historical underground railroad.

40 "Clues to Creativity in Written Expression." *Report of Instructional Research Institute on Written English.* Westbrook, CT: State Department of Education (sponsored jointly by the Boards of Education in Haddam, Lyme, Middlefield, Salem, and Westbrook), 1966.

Petry shares what she calls "two unforgettable experiences" with two former English teachers in her response to "how to recognize creative writers, how to encourage them, and how to foster talent" in the classroom. The writer suggests to educators that they begin by getting "youngsters to think with their own minds."

41 "The Common Ground." *The Horn Book Magazine* 41 (April 1965): 141–151. Also appears in *Horn Book Reflections*. Edited by Elinor W. Field. Boston: Horn Book, 1969.

Petry reveals why she wrote *Harriet Tubman, Conductor on the Underground Railroad* and *Tituba of Salem Village*.

42 "David in Silence." *New York Times Book Review,* 8 May 1966, 32.

Petry reviews briefly Veronica Robinson's *David in Silence,* a short novel about a deaf youth from England who gains for himself hard-won respect.

43 "Doomed Boys May Live Due to Layman's Plea." *People's Voice,* 26 June 1943, 13.

Reports that clemency may be granted to three Puerto Rican youths who had been found guilty of murdering a soldier while he sought a prostitute in the youths' neighborhood.

44 "The Great Secret." *The Writer* 61 (July 1948): 215–217.

Analogies are used by the writer to explain how she wrote her first two novels. The writer equates herself with a shoemaker and a mechanic, both needing specific tools in order to accomplish their jobs. Petry's tools are the following: "words; a better-than-average knowledge of people; and a first-class story-telling technique."

45 "Harlem." *Holiday* (April 1949): 110–116, 163–166, 168.

This essay is Petry's descriptive account of Harlem's "thousand varied faces"—from aspiring Sugar Hill to the desolate Hollows. Photographs depict how the wealthy and the poor live.

46 "Harlem Urged to Attend First Meeting of Women, Inc." *People's Voice,* 2 May 1942, 17.

Announces the first meeting of Women, Inc., a consumer information and action group in Harlem. Includes an agenda that addresses the concerns of women interested in themselves and in Harlem as a place in which to live "during the war and after the war is over."

47 "Harlem Woman Wax Indignant Over Latest 'Crime' Campaign." *People's Voice,* 15 August 1942, 3.

Polls the opinions of "Negro" women from Harlem about an article carried in the white-owned *Daily News.* The article told of how white soldiers were being barred from Harlem because of prostitution among Harlem's black women.

48 "I, Juan De Pareja." *New York Times Book Review,* 22 August 1965, 18.

A brief book review of Elizabeth Borton de Trevino's *I, Juan de Pareja*—a historical novel about a slave named Pareja who wins his freedom from his Spanish master, the artist Velazquez, after gaining recognition himself as a talented artist.

49 "The Lighter Side" (weekly column). *People's Voice,* 7 March 1942–8 May 1943.

Weekly column that focuses on art, literature, music, and "who's who" in middle-class black America. Like Addison and Steele in their eighteenth-century *The Spectator* or Samuel Johnson in *The Rambler,* Miss Smith and Miss Jones, creations of Petry, commented on various issues in "The Lighter Side."

50 "Miss Halsey Feelingly Records an Interracial Experiment." *PM* (22 September 1946): 15.

A book review of Margaret Halsey's *Color Blind.* Petry says Halsey has done an "enormous service for both Negroes and whites," particularly in her study of interracial relations at the Stage Door Canteen—a nondiscriminatory social club for servicemen located off Broadway in the 1940s.

51 "The New American Outlaws." *Saturday Review of Literature* (23 December 1950): 21.

A book review of Philip B. Kaye's *Taffy*—a novel about a male protagonist named Taffy who grows up in Harlem and becomes a hoodlum and a murderer by age eighteen. Petry contrasts the strong characterizations of Taffy and his gang to the weak characterizations of Taffy's law-abiding family.

52 "New England's John Henry." *Negro Digest* 3, no. 5 (March 1945): 71–73.

Legends, anecdotes, and quotations help make up a portrait of New England's own John Henry—Venture Smith. Once a slave who labored with his own nine-pound axe, Smith bought his freedom, a shipping business, and rich fertile land in New England.

53 "No Mobs, No Fiery Crosses." *New York Herald Tribune Weekly Book Review,* 10 April 1949, 4.

A book review of Bucklin Moon's *Without Magnolias.* Petry disapproves of Moon's "downplay" of "real drama" in everyday life. She concludes, however, that the novel paints an "accurate, realistic picture" of the "delicate balance of race relations in the South," and that it presents recognizable characters.

54 "The Novel as Social Criticism." In *The Writer's Book.* Edited by Helen Hull. New York: Harper and Brothers, 1950.

Petry argues against the idea that the novel becomes less art and more propaganda when it is used to serve moral or political ends. She says the novel will "always" reflect the economic, social, and political times in which it is created. For Petry, the socially conscious novelist is merely "a man or a woman with a conscience." She praises the novel of social criticism and concludes that it has aroused interest in social reforms, even the passage of civil rights legislation.

55 "Race Betrayal." *Saturday Review of Literature* (25 February 1950): 18.
    A book review of J. Saunders Redding's *Stranger and Alone.* Petry proclaims that the novel "evokes pity and terror." She calls central character Sheldon Howden "more frightening than a lynch victim." As superintendent of New York's black schools, Howden responds to unwritten codes that governed relations between blacks and whites and reinforced the theory that members of his race were inferior to whites.

56 Review of *Youngblood. New York Herald Tribune Book Review,* 11 July 1954, 8.
    Reviews briefly John Oliver Killens's' *Youngblood.* Approves of good development of the major and minor characters. However, disapproves of scenes of racially inspired violence as too repetitive.

57 "System of Control Is not Intricate." *People's Voice,* 9 January 1943, 6.
    Explains how to use the special ration book issued by the Office of Price Administration (OPA) of the United States government in the 1940s.

58 "This Writing Business." *Author's Guild Bulletin* [Special Collections, Boston University], 1965.
    Miscellaneous comments on Petry.

59 "Tribute to Mr. Gentry." *Connecticut Pharmacist.* 3 (November 1946): 5, 42.
    An imaginary druggist named Mr. Gentry symbolizes all small-town druggists. His actions suggest that the contributions of the small-town druggist range from medical to social to political.

60 "Tubman, Harriet." *Encyclopaedia Britannica,* vol. 22, 1970, 302.
    A biographical sketch of the black female abolitionist and activist Harriet Tubman. As the "Moses" of her people, Tubman successfully guides over 300 slaves from bondage in the United States to freedom in Canada.

61 "U.S. Will Fail as World Leader If Ruled by Jimcro—Mrs. F. D. R." *People's Voice,* 8 May 1943, 7.
    Covers a lecture–concert sponsored by the New York City Committee to honor Mrs. Mary McLeod Bethune and to benefit Bethune-Cookman College. Guest lecturer is Mrs. Franklin Delano Roosevelt. Quotes Mrs. Roosevelt as having said Mrs. Bethune "symbolizes a spirit of courage, love, endurance and hope that is very necessary in the present world." In terms of race relations in the 1940s in the United States, Mrs. Roosevelt is

quoted as saying "prejudice is due to ignorance and lack of education." She concludes that the country has an opportunity to lead at the present time but will fail as a leader if it is controlled by ignorance.

62   "What's Wrong with Negro Men?" *Negro Digest* 5, no. 5 (March 1947): 4–7.
     Petry's point of view is satirical. She concludes that the male attitudes discussed in her article come straight out of the Dark Ages.

Secondary Works

63 Adams, George. "Riot as Ritual: Ann Petry's 'In Darkness and Confusion.'" *Black American Literature Forum* 6, no. 2 (Summer 1972): 54–58.

Provides thematic and archetypical readings of the short story. Outlines how when a riot breaks out protagonist William is "born again through sacrifices" and through the "ritualized shedding of the past."

64 Adams, William, Peter Conn, and Barry Slepian, eds. *Afro-American Literature: Fiction.* Boston: Houghton Mifflin, 1970.

Provides an excerpt from *The Street* under the subtitle "The Family." The excerpt is followed by study questions.

65 Alexander, Sandra Carlton. Ann Petry. In *Dictionary of Literary Biography: Afro-American Writers. 1940–1955.* Vol. 6. Edited by Trudier Harris. Detroit: Gale Research, 1988.

Insists Petry is a "study in contrast" and that she demonstrates versatility in her writings about urban and New England rural lives of African-Americans. With the exception of "The Common Ground," which is erroneously listed as a book, the writer provides accurate chronological listings of Petry's fiction and juvenile works. Includes summaries of plots and, in some instances, critical character analyses.

66 Angelou, Maya. *Black Women Writers at Work.* Edited by Claudia Tate. New York: Continuum, 1983.

Pays tribute to Petry. Angelou says she would walk "fifty blocks in high heels" for something written by Petry (p. 60).

67 "Ann Petry Gets Warm Reception at Book Fair." *Hampton Bulletin* (January 1956): 3.

Speaking at the first all-community Book Bazaar at Hampton Institute (now University), Petry advises prospective writers to practice self-discipline and to read. She suggests "liberal reading, but with emphasis upon the Greek tragedies, the Bible, and the great works of 18th Century Western Europe."

68 "Ann Petry Tells Parley of Need for Play Schools." *New York Herald Tribune Book Review,* 14 April 1946, 5.

Identifies Petry's role as a recreation specialist in Harlem's Play Schools Association, which provides community programs for minority parents and their children.

69 "Ann Petry's New Book Tells Story of a Heroic Negro Woman Who Led Slaves to Freedom." *New Era* (29 September 1955): 1.

Review of *Harriet Tubman, Conductor of the Underground Railroad.* Calls the work "absorbing" reading and more than a "factual biography." Petry is applauded for her "delicate" and "evocative" words that help recreate "the fear of being sold into deeper misery" and "the hopeless insecurity of the slaves' lives." Tubman is said to be "a living figure" in this work.

70 "Ann Petry's 'The Street' Is Sugar-Coated Problem Novel." *Afro-American* (Baltimore), 2 February 1946, 14.

Announces the February release of *The Street* and quotes Petry's reasons for writing the novel.

71 "An Interview with Ann Petry." *Artspectrum* (Windham–Regional Arts Council, Willimantic, CT), September 1988, 3–4.

Poses familiar questions. Two exceptions, however, concern Petry's role as a feminist and her position on the civil rights movement. [See full interview in this bibliography.]

72 Ann Petry. In *African American Literature, Voices in a Tradition.* Orlando, FL: Holt, Rinehart and Winston, 1992.

A textbook first introduced in secondary schools in cities such as Detroit and Memphis. Provided in the text are African-American literary maps, history and literary terms, chronological listings of African-American literature from the beginning to present, thematic approaches to writers, photographs of African artifacts and of well-known African-Americans, and paintings by African-American artists. Unit Six ("From Renaissance to Mid-Forties") includes opening paragraphs from Petry's *The Street.* Discussion questions follow. A 1946 photograph of Petry is provided.

73 Ann Petry. In *Black Writers.* Senior editor, Linda Metzger. Detroit: Gale Research, 1989.

A chronological listing of Petry's first three novels and excerpts from book reviews, dating from the 1940s to the 1970s.

74 Ann Petry. In *Contemporary Authors.* Edited by Barbara Harte and Carolyn Riley. Vols. 5–8. Detroit: Gale Research, 1963. Reprint. 1969.

Provides vital statistics on Petry, her hobbies, and an abbreviated listing of her writings.

75 Ann Petry. In *Contemporary Authors: Autobiography Series.* Vol. 6. Detroit: Gale Research, 1988.

    Petry calls herself a survivor in the literary sense and an advocate of children's literature. Introduces family photographs. Offers comments on her novels.

76 Ann Petry. In *Contemporary Literary Criticism.* Edited by Carolyn Riley. Detroit, Gale Research, 1973.

    Provides literary analysis of *Country Place* and stories from *Miss Muriel and Other Stories.* Quotes Carl Milton Hughes, Robert Bone, Alfred Kazin, and Houston Baker, Jr.

77 Ann Petry. In *Contemporary Literary Criticism.* Edited by Phyllis Carmel Mendelson and Dedria Bryfonski. Detroit: Gale Research, 1977.

    Presents excerpts of critical writings on Petry's style and structure in her short and long fiction. Quotes David Littlejohn, Thelma J. Shinn, and William Peden.

78 Ann Petry. In *Contemporary Literary Criticism.* Edited by Sharon R. Gunton. Vol. 18. Detroit: Gale Research, 1981.

    Reprints excerpts from reviews of *Country Place, The Narrows,* and the short shory "In Darkness and Confusion," by Authur P. Davis, Arna Bontemps, and George R. Adams respectively.

79 Ann Petry. In *Current Biography.* Edited by Anna Rothe. New York: H. W. Wilson, 1946.

    Provides a biographical sketch and the phonetic spelling of the writer's surname, which is with a long "e" (pee-tree). Photograph included.

80 Ann Petry. In *Dictionary of American Children's Fiction, 1960–1984.* Edited by Alethea K. Helbig, and Agnes Regan Perkins. New York: Greenwood, 1986.

    Acknowledges Petry's biographies for youth (*Harriet Tubman* and *Tituba of Salem Village*), yet provides extensive plot summary for only *Tituba.* Calls the narrative structure of *Tituba* brief, saying that it summarizes events, particularly following the trial of Tituba.

81 Ann Petry. In *Harlem Renaissance and Beyond.* Edited by Lorraine Elena Roses and Ruth Elizabeth Randolph. Boston: G. K. Hall, 1990.

    Calls Petry a "bridge figure between the Harlem Renaissance and the black writers after mid century." Considers Petry a precursor to Toni Morrison and Gloria Naylor. Says that contrary to "forced" comparisons between the best-sellers by Richard Wright and Chester Himes of the 1940s, *The Street* has "a poetic breadth all its own." Offers answers to "why critics are made so uncomfortable by Petry's works."

82 Ann Petry. In *Historical Negro Biographies* by Wilhelmina S. Robinson. New York: Publishers Co. Inc. [under the auspices of The Association for the Study of Negro Life and History], 1967.

Provides a brief biography of Petry, with errors.

83 Ann Petry. In *Interviews with Black Writers.* Edited by John O'Brien. New York: Liveright, 1973.

Discusses the author's craft with her. See full interview in this bibliography.

84 Ann Petry. In *Portraits in Color.* Edited by Gwendolyn Cherry, Ruby Thomas, and Pauline Willis. New York: Pageant, 1962.

Comparisons between Petry and earlier writers of so-called problem novels to show how Petry differs, particularly when in *The Street* or *Country Place* she presents a "strong story line, brilliant characterization, and fast-moving plot."

85 Ann Petry. In *Reader's Encyclopedia of American Literature.* Edited by Max Herzberg. New York: Thomas Y. Crowell, 1962.

An abbreviated biography and listing of her novels. Calls *The Street* the "best ever written about Harlem."

86 Ann Petry. In *The Chelsea House Library of Literary Criticism: Twentieth Century American Literature.* General Editor Harold Bloom. Vol. 5 (M–P). New York: Chelsea House, 1987.

Provides criticism of Petry's craft in excerpts from the following: David Littlejohn's *Black on White,* Robert Bone's *The Negro Novel in America,* and Arthur P. Davis's *From the Dark Tower.*

87 Ann Petry. In *Twentieth Century Authors: A Biographical Dictionary of Modern Literature.* Edited by Stanley J. Kunitz. New York: H. W. Wilson, 1955.

Offers quotes by the author on her biography and bibliography. Reveals that the author's surname is pronounced with a long "e" (pee-tree).

88 "A Visit with Ann Petry." College of Pharmacy, University of Illinois at Chicago. Deposited in Kremers Reference Files. Madison: University of Wisconsin School of Pharmacy, 1984.

An intriguing conversation/interview between Petry and pharmacy students at the University of Illinois at Chicago. [Interview appears in this bibliography.]

89 Baker, Henry. "Witchcraft: The Idea Is Both Old and Modern." *Middletown Press,* 6 January 1970 [Special Collections, Boston University].

Summarizes Petry's speech at a meeting held by the Old Saybrook Historical Society. Presents data Petry collected during her research on witchcraft.

90 Baker, Houston A., Jr., ed. Overview. In *Black Literature in America*. New York: McGraw-Hill, 1971.

Discusses Petry in his Overview. Calls her characters "complex human beings." Concludes that Petry writes unflinchingly in a "realistic tradition." Includes reprint of "Like a Winding Sheet."

91 Balliett, Whitney. "Imagining Music." *New Yorker* (18 June 1990): 93–94.

Mentions favorably Petry's "Solo on the Drums" in this study of how jazz novelists imagine the music. Concludes that Petry's "jilted drummer makes his 'big boss' drum growl."

92 Bartter, George C. Review of *The Street*. *Book Find News* 2 (April 1946): 16.

Writes that *The Street* is "a rich, smooth-flowing novel filled with people you know and understand." Rejects criticism that Petry's characters are criminals.

93 Bell, Bernard W. "Ann Petry's Demythologizing of American Culture and Afro-American Character." In *Conjuring: Black Women, Fiction, and Literary Tradition*. Edited by Marjorie Pryse and Hortense J. Spillers. Bloomington: Indiana University Press, 1985.

Writes that Petry moves "beyond the naturalistic vision of Wright and Himes" when she explores "the black community's place in time and space [and] its relationship to the American past and future." Concludes that because of Petry's "realistic delineation of cultural myths," she "debunks the myths of urban success and progress, of rural innocence and virtue, and of pathological black women and men."

94 ———. "The Triumph of Naturalism." In *The Afro-American Novel and Its Tradition*. Amherst: University of Massachusetts Press, 1987. Reprint. 1989.

Insists Petry's "most invaluable achievement in the tradition of the Afro-American novel" is her successful move "beyond the naturalistic vision of Himes and Wright to a demythologizing of American culture and Afro-American character."

95 Bell, Roseann P., Bettye J. Parker, and Beverly Guy-Sheftall, eds. *Sturdy Black Bridges: Visions of Black Women in Literature*. Garden City, NY: Anchor/Doubleday, 1979.

Reprints Petry's interview with James Ivy. Writes that when in *The Street* Lutie murders her would-be rapist, Boots, Petry redeems Richard Wright's victimized Bessie, and she revises Wright's Bigger Thomas. Says that "out of necessity," African-American women novelists are turning not to male writers for encouragement and mentoring but to role models like Petry.

96 Benoit, Larry. "Introducing Two Small-Town Druggists," 1946 [Special Collections, Boston University].

Focuses on how Petry's father, Peter C. Lane, got his start as a druggist. Highlights the contributions of Petry's aunt, Miss Anna L. James, who was also a druggist.

97 Bixler, Paul. "Freedom Takes Time." *Antioch Review* 7, no. 2 (1946): 269–74.

Compares Petry's "limited intrusion" and "objectivity" with Richard Wright's intrusive voice and his indicting tone in *Native Son*. Concludes that because Petry knew considerable security in her life and had not been subjected to Lutie's "way of living all her life," she was horrified at what she saw in Harlem and was "able to translate" her horror "straight . . . into terms . . . instantly recognized and widely understood." Compares Petry briefly with Zola.

98 ———. "She Tried to Flee Harlem: Tragic Tale in the Great Tradition of Naturalism." *Chicago Sun Book Week,* 10 February 1946 [Special Collections, Woodruff, Atlanta University Center].

Writes that neither Zola, Dreiser, nor James Farrell had material "better fitted to the naturalistic hand." Refutes others critics' labeling of Petry's characters as simply evil. Says "environment and the urge to survive" help shape their behaviors. Bixler criticizes the middle of the novel, calling its intent "unsure" and its pace "uneven." Concludes, however, with favorable comments. Says novel is "one of the most powerful . . . of the past decade."

99 Bone, Robert. "Black Writing in the 1970s." *Nation* 227 (16 December 1978): 677–679.

Identifies important trends in major African-American writings in the 1970s. Under the short story, he includes Petry's *Miss Muriel and Other Stories,* calling her stories "outstanding."

100 ———. *The Negro Novel in America.* New Haven: Yale University Press, 1958. Revised. 1965.

Calls Petry a disciple of Richard Wright and *The Street* an "environmentalist" novel. Believes the novel, however, lacks the "historical sweep" of the synthesization of racial and social protest found in Wright's *Native Son.* Bone favors *Country Place* for its "forceful characterization," its "tight and economical style," and its "well-executed design." Classifies *Country Place* as the "best" of the assimilationist novels.

101 Bontemps, Arna. "Awakening." In *Story of the Negro.* New York: Knopf, 1969.

Provides explanations for the shaping of twentieth-century ideology in African-American art and literature. Cites Petry as a successful mainstream artist.

102 ———. "The Line." *Saturday Review of Literature* (22 August 1953): 11.
Says Petry elects to be a "neighborhood novelist" in her controlled yet "electrifying" *The Narrows.* Suggests Petry's style is New England.

103 ———. "Tough, Carnal Harlem." *New York Herald Tribune Weekly Book Review,* 10 February 1946, 4.
Calls Petry an "unblushing realist" who "leaves out none of the essential character" of the street.

104 Brock, Sabine, ed. "'The Street'—Kein Ort. Nirgends." *Der entkolonisierte Korper, Die Protagonistin in der afroamerikanischen weiblichen Erzahltradition der 30er bis 80er Jahre (The Decolonized Body, The Female Protagonist in the Afro-American Woman's Narrative Tradition from the 1930s to the 1980s).* New York: Campus Verlag, 1988.
Writing in German, Brock adds to Petry's title "Kein Ort. Nirgends," which means "No place. No where." Says *The Street* suggests that the mainstream dream from the woman's perspective is impossible because society does not offer a place for black women. Calls Petry the "sharpest contrast" to Zora Neale Hurston and Paule Marshall.

105 Brown, Lloyd W. "Tituba of Barbados and the American Conscience: Historical Perspectives in Arthur Miller and Ann Petry." *Caribbean Studies* 13, no. 4 (January 1974): 118–126.
Compares and contrasts Arthur Miller's *Crucible* and Petry's *Tituba of Salem Village* because of their "major" treatments of Tituba Indian, a slave woman accused during the seventeenth century of being a witch. Concludes that Petry's treatment of Tituba's situation is ethical and social, and that her drawing of Tituba's character is convincingly human.

106 Brown, Sterling A. "A Century of Negro Portraiture in American Literature." *Massachusetts Review* 7, no. 1 (Winter 1966): 73–96. Also in *Black and White in American Culture: An Anthology from the Massachusetts Review.* Edited by Jules Chametzky and Sidney Kaplan. Amherst: University of Massachusetts, 1969. *Black Voices.* Edited by Abraham Chapman. New York: New American Library, 1968.
Includes Petry in his compilation of literary history on African-American literature. Calls *The Street* an "authentic" slice of Harlem life and a refutation of the exotic.

107 Brown, Thomasine Corbett. "Elements of Naturalism in Ann Petry's *The Street.*" Master's thesis, University of North Carolina at Chapel Hill, 1966.
Uses reviews and critical studies of *The Street* to support her thesis that naturalistic qualities exist in the novel, yet insists the novel is also artistic. Discusses separately elements of the novel (plot, setting, point of view, characters, and theme) and how naturalistic and artistic qualities apply to each.

108   Buell, Ellen Lewis. "A Tempery Cat." *New York Times Book Review,*
      6 November 1949, 24.
          Provides a very brief summary of what is called "a beguiling story which
      catches the essence of kitten nature." Criticizes the illustrator for her pictures,
      which sometimes do not accompany the story line in *The Drugstore Cat.*

109   ———. "The Deliverer." *New York Times Book Review,* 16 October
      1955, 34.
          Reviews *Harriet Tubman, Conductor on the Underground Railroad.*
      Calls the work insightful and stylish. Considers the brief historical sum-
      maries that appear at the end of each chapter to be assets. Compares Petry's
      biography to an earlier work by Dorothy Sterling ("Railroad to Freedom"),
      concluding that Petry's work is "more introspective."

110   Buncombe, Marie H. "From Harlem to Brooklyn: The New York Scene in
      the Fiction of Meriwether, Petry, and Marshall." *MAWA Review* 1, no. 1
      (Spring 1982): 16–19.
          Discusses *The Street, Daddy Was a Number Runner,* and *Brown Girl,
      Brownstones* as a trilogy and concludes that from this trilogy come two ma-
      jor purposes of setting: the setting records history of blacks in New York
      City, particularly working-class black women in Harlem and in boroughs
      like Brooklyn who have had to swallow their pride, face reality, and get
      jobs. Setting also serves as a "tarnished symbol" of that "land of opportu-
      nity"—America.

111   Burns, Ben. "Off the Book Shelf." *Chicago Defender* 9 February 1946
      [Special Collections, Boston University].
          Defines "the street" as an "octopus-like monster" and as "one of the
      most terrible villains ever described in a book." Petry is said to approach her
      characters "with the penetration of a psychiarist and the delicate care of a
      mother." The mood and tempo in *The Street* is said to be comparable to the
      mood and tempo in Edgar Allan Poe's "Pit and the Pendulum." Petry is also
      said to have avoided one shortcoming that marred Richard Wright's *Native
      Son*—melodrama.

112   Butcher, Margaret Just. "Regional Nationalism in American Culture." In
      The Negro in American Culture [based on materials left by Alain Locke].
      New York: Knopf, 1968.
          Names Petry along with a list of male writers (Richard Wright, Willard
      Motley, Ralph Ellison, and James Baldwin) for achieving universal charac-
      ters through people "who simply happen to be colored."

113   ———. "The Negro in Modern American Fiction." In *The Negro in American
      Culture* [based on materials left by Alain Locke]. New York: Knopf, 1968.
          Mentions Petry favorably and cites her novels *The Street* and *Country
      Place.*

114 Butcher, Philip. "Our Raceless Writers." *Opportunity: Journal of Negro Life* 26, no. 3 (July–September 1948): 113–115.

Traces the tradition of raceless novels by African-American writers. Includes in his discussion Petry's *Country Place.* Offers a brief review of the work, calling it a "study of the deteriorating small town." Also points out Petry's carelessness: Johnnie gets in the front of the Weazel's cab, but he is viewed by the Weazel through the rearview mirror. Also criticizes Petry's varying point of view.

115 Butterfield, Alfred. "The Dark Heartbeat of Harlem." *New York Times Book Review,* 10 February 1946, 6.

Referring to *The Street,* calls Lutie's struggle against her own race and neighborhood while attempting to provide a safe and comfortable home for herself and her son a "personal epic."

116 Cahill, Susan, ed. *Women and Fiction.* New York: New American Library, 1975.

In this collection of twenty-six short stories of women writers, Cahill includes Petry's "Like a Winding Sheet" because of its "vision and craft." Suggests that Petry's story can be compared with Edith Wharton's "A Worn Path" and Katherine Anne Porter's "Rope."

117 Chambers, Bradford, and Rebecca Moon, eds. *Right On! An Anthology of Black Literature.* New York: New American Library, 1970.

Includes Petry's short story "In Darkness and Confusion" under a section entitled "Oppression." Calls the work an example of a "modern urban ghetto."

118 Chandler, Zala. "Interview with Toni Cade Bambara and Sonia Sanchez." In *Wild Women in the Whirlwind: Afra-American Culture and the Contemporary Literary Renaissance.* Edited by Joanne M. Braxton and Andree Nicola McLaughlin. New Brunswick, NJ: Rutgers University Press, 1990.

Sanchez names Petry, among other women writers, as an inspiration to her in the literary tradition. Says because of Petry and others, she can "feel" history.

119 Christian, Barbara T. *From the Inside Out: Afro-American Women's Literary Tradition and the State.* CHS Occasional Papers, Number 19. Minneapolis: University of Minnesota, Center for Humanistic Studies, 1987.

Taking her title from a line in June Jordan's "Declaration of an Independence I Would Just as Soon Not Have," Christian identifies several African-American women writers who deny essential aspects of black womanhood in their writings in order to fit others' definitions, and others who define black womanhood via codes or subversions in their writings. [For discussion of subversions in Petry's texts, see Ervin, Number 161 in this bibliography.] In a later discussion of the political significance of contemporary African-American women writers, Christian briefly mentions Petry for her emphasis in *The Street* on the effect of the "conditions of poverty and oppression on black women."

120 ———. "Images of Black Women in Afro-American Literature: From Stereotype to Character (1975)." In *Black Feminist Criticism: Perspectives on Black Women Writers*. New York: Pergamon, 1985. Reprint. 1989.

Calls *The Street* functional in its capacity to displace the typical tragic mulatto with a complex, urban heroine but thinks that Lutie brings with her certain stereotypes: the "domestic worker"; the "struggling single mother"; and the "tragic mulatto." Concludes, however, that Petry's setting and tone help to bring the literature by African-American women into the twentieth century.

121 ———. "Ordinary Women: The Tone of the Commonplace." In *Black Women Novelists: The Development of a Tradition, 1892–1976*. Westport, CT: Greenwood, 1980.

Writes that in *The Street,* there is a tone of the commonplace: "a selection of details and seemingly trivial struggles that poor women can seldom avoid." Recognizes *The Street* as one of the first novels to present a "struggling urban black mother attempting to create a better life for herself." Compares Petry's novel to previous publications by both African-American women and men writers.

122 Clark, Graham. "Beyond Realism: Recent Black Fiction and the Language of 'The Real Thing.'" In *Black Fiction: New Studies in the Afro-American Novel Since 1946*. Edited by A. Robert Lee. New York: Barnes and Noble, 1980.

Focuses on fiction after 1957 and its consciously "black modernist voice." However, goes back to refute Robert Bone's denouncement of "tired and worn racial prescriptions" in African-American writings after *Native Son*. Suggests that Bone's call for a "new style"—most obvious in a consciously black modernist voice—was being developed "in precisely that tradition of Afro-American realist writing[s] which Bone saw as so worn and frenzied"— mainly in writings by Petry and the early works of Chester Himes.

123 Clark, Keith. "A Distaff Dream Deferred? Ann Petry and the Art of Subversion." *African-American Review* 26, no. 3 (Fall 1992): 495–505.

Provides a post–structuralist reading of *The Street.*

124 Clark, Sidney. "Amoral Lives." *Hartford Courant,* 23 August 1953 [Special Collections, Boston University].

Calls for the Pulitzer Prize for Petry's "love story" in *The Narrows.* Provides a plot summary and very brief characterizations of Abbie Crunch and Mamie Powther, calling both women the "amoral individuals" who endure and survive. Also draws a very brief comparison between Abbie Crunch and Faulkner's Lena Groves in *Light in August.*

125 Clarke, Cheryl. "Ann Petry and the Isolation of Being Other." *Belles Lettres*
5 (Fall 1989): 36.
    Intersperses comments with facts and quotes gathered from correspon-
dence with the writer and from an autobiographical essay by Petry. Encourages readers to read Petry's short stories collected in *Miss Muriel and Other
Stories.*

126 Clarke, John Henrik, ed. Introduction. *Harlem.* New York: Signet/New
American Library, 1970.
    Writes in his introduction that Petry captures the many "moods" of
Harlem. Calls Petry "one of the best present-day craftsmen" of the short
story. Includes in this collection "In Darkness and Confusion."

127 Clemmons, Lucy Lee. "Grime, Garbage and Ugliness." *Phylon* 7, no. 1
(First Quarter 1946): 98–99.
    Writes that "despite the sordidness, the squalor, [and] the bitterness,
there is a fundamental understanding of basic human qualities and realism"
concerning African-American life in *The Street.*

128 Coffey, Michael. "Black Writers Debate 'Being Human in the 20th Century' (5th Annual Celebration of Black Writing)." *Publishers' Weekly* (17
February 1989): 17.
    Mentions briefly that Ann Petry is guest of honor at the Fifth Annual
Black Writers' Conference and is also honored later in the evening at a reception at the Free Library of Philadelphia. Photograph of Petry is included.

129 "Color and Conflict." *The Times* (London), 27 August 1954 [Special Collections, Boston University].
    Reviews *The Narrows.* States that Petry represents the new African-
American writer who is able to examine her race, its characteristics, and
problems "without the underlying current of resentment." Says that *The
Narrows* has familiar defects and qualities of the Wolfe–Faulkner school—
"poetry, rhetoric, diffuseness and colour."

130 "Color in Connecticut." *Time* (17 August 1953): 94, 96.
    Proposes that the setting in *The Narrows* is most "remarkable," espe-
cially when compared to other elements in the novel. Says plot is seriously
told, but prefers the "rich parallel story" of Malcolm Powther. Predicts that
Malcolm and Mamie Powther's story will help to sustain *The Narrows,*
more so than the "fictional survival" of Link Williams and Camilo Sheffield.

131 "Commentary." In *The World of Fiction.* Edited by David Madden.
Chicago: Holt, Rinehart and Winston, 1990.
    Comments on Petry's literary strategies in her short story "The Wit-
ness," particularly her point of view, characterization, and theme. "The
Witness" is reprinted, followed by questions and "writing suggestions."

132 Conrad, Earl. "A Woman's Place in Harlem." *Chicago Defender,* 2 February 1946, 13.

   Concludes that Petry, as both the award-winning novelist and a wife, is the "most apt symbol" of the African-American question concerning the woman's place. Petry discusses the status of the African-American woman, both in literature and in the real world, and her own efforts in *The Street* to portray women more realistically.

133 *Contributions of Black Women to America (The Arts, Media, Business, Law, Sports).* Edited by Marianna W. Davis. Vol. 1. Columbia, SC: Kenday, 1982.

   Pays tribute to Petry for her fiction. Includes a picture, courtesy of *Ebony.*

134 Cooke, Michael. "Introduction: Building on 'Signifying' and the Blues." *Afro-American Literature in the Twentieth Century: The Achievement of Intimacy.* New Haven: Yale University Press, 1984.

   Moves African-American literature outside of "signifying" the blues. Contends that there are "four major modes and stages" in the literature: self-veiling, solitude, kinship, and intimacy. Petry's protagonist Lutie is included in the section on solitude.

135 Corbett, Jane. "Store Porch Gossip." *Times Educational Supplement,* 19 September 1986, 40.

   Acknowledges the literary contributions of Zora Neale Hurston and Ann Petry to African-American literature.

136 Cosgrave, Mary Silva. "In Tune with Their Times." *Book Week* 2 (1 November 1964): 28.

   Concludes *Tituba of Salem Village* is "in tune" with the seventeenth-century Salem witch trials in America. The reviewer says Petry's work is reminiscent of Elizabeth George Speare's *The Witch of Blackbird Pond.*

137 Crane, Mary Ellen. "Life in Harlem." *Birmingham News* 9 March 1946 [Special Collections, Boston University].

   Notes "wonderous personalities" that emerge in *The Street* due to characters' relationships to "the street," particularly Min, who is thought to be "the most successful portrait of them all." Applauds Petry's "treatment of loneliness in cities" and Lutie's "struggle to prove the existence of free will."

138 Currier, Isabel. "'The Street' is Realistic Literature." *Boston Herald,* 20 February 1946 [Special Collections, Boston University].

   Insists *The Street* is "as unpretty as the horror films from Germany's mass-murder concentration camps." Says it is the "painful duty" of all who earnestly seek peace to read this novel. Criticism is also directed toward Petry's lack of balance for truth: her story "has only one dimension"; her "prose spills out in colloquial violence"; her characters other than Lutie are "dwarfed by the monstrosities of their separate and collective natures."

139 Curtis, Constance. Review of *The Street. Amsterdam News* (New York), 16 February 1946 [Special Collections, Woodruff, Atlanta University Center].
Praises the work, but not without calling attention to the wordiness of its style and its melodramatic conclusion.

140 Daltry, Patience M. Review of *Tituba of Salem Village. Christian Science Monitor,* 25 February 1965, 7.
Contends that Petry contrasts Christianity as practiced by a slave from Barbados who is tried for witchcraft and by a rigid sect of Puritans in the 1600s in Salem. Concludes that Petry combines reality and fiction to produce a vivid story.

141 Dandridge, Rita B. "Male Critics/Black Women's Novels." *CLA Journal* 23, no. 1 (September 1979): 1–2.
Discloses how male critics review novels by African-American women writers with "apathy, chauvinism, and paternalism" and cites as an example David Littlejohn's discussion of Petry and Richard Wright, James Baldwin, and Ralph Ellison in *Black on White.* Dandridge applauds Petry's "creative sympathy."

142 Daniel, Thomas H. "Street in Harlem is Subject of New Book." *Columbia Record* (South Carolina), 7 February 1946 [Special Collections, Boston University].
Calls *The Street* "a faithful portrayal of a segment of American life" that is not necessarily limited to African-Americans. Calls Petry's style "Dickensian," particularly her emphasis on the temptations and struggles of Lutie in an environment filled with "poverty, degradation, and crime."

143 Davis, Arthur P. "Integrationists and Transitional Writers." In *From the Dark Tower: Afro-American Writers, 1900 to 1960.* Washington, DC: Howard University Press, 1974.
Provides literary analysis of all three of Petry's novels. Mentions her literary strengths in her children's works and in her collections of short stories. Overall, considers Petry a "competent" writer—that is, she "does several things well, but none superlatively." Believes Petry's short stories will "stand up best after the critical years have passed judgment."

144 ———. "Negro American Literature." In *Negro Year Book: A Review of Events Affecting Negro Life 1941–1946.* Edited by Jessie Parkhurst Guzman. Tuskegee, AL: Department of Records and Research, Tuskegee Institute, 1947.
Begins with a background discussion of the Harlem Renaissance. Discusses effects of the movement on the "hard-boiled writers," including

Petry, of the Chicago Renaissance. Considers Petry's *The Street* a "milder [and] less powerful New York version of *Native Son.*"

145 ———. Review of *The Street. Journal of Negro Education* 15, no. 4 (Fall 1946): 649.

Applauds *The Street* for its sound thesis and its universal appeal. Criticizes the novel for its melodramatic characterizations of Junto and Mrs. Hedges and also its "forced ending."

146 Davis, Arthur P., J. Saunders Redding, and Joyce Ann Joyce, eds. *New Cavalcade: African-American Writing from 1760 to Present.* Vol. 1. Washington, DC: Howard University Press, 1991.

Provides a brief biographical sketch. Reprints "Like a Winding Sheet."

147 Davis, Arthur P., and J. Saunders Redding, eds. *Cavalcade: Negro American Writing from 1760 to the Present.* Boston: Houghton Mifflin, 1971.

Renames an excerpt from *The Street* "Dead End Street." Calls the novel "one of the better . . . of the naturalistic school."

148 Davis, Carole Boyce, ed. "Black Women's Writing: Crossing the Boundaries." *Matatu: Zeitschrift fur Afrikanische und Gesellschaft* 3, no. 6 (1989): 1–4.

Includes Petry in her discussion of black women writers.

149 Davis, Thulani. "Family Plots: Black Women Writers Reclaim Their Past." *The Village Voice* 32, no. 10 (10 March 1987): 14–17.

Responding to critics who suggest that contemporary African-American women writers have "broken a silent pact among all African-American writers to present positive images and to critic Mel Watkins (*New York Times Book Review,* 15 June 1986), who traces "the portrayal of hostility between black men and women to a 1967 novel [*The Flagellants*] by Carlene Hatcher Polite," Davis returns to early African-American novelists, or "motherlodes," like Jessie Fauset, Nella Larsen, Zora Neale Hurston, and Ann Petry to show that the impulses and concerns of these writers often parallel those of contemporary African-American women writers. She concludes that together the "motherlodes" and the contemporary women writers help to create the "black women's tradition within the larger black literary tradition."

150 Demarest, David P., and Lois S. Lamdin, eds. *The Ghetto Reader.* New York: Random House, 1970.

Includes an excerpt from *The Street* entitled "Bub and Ben Franklin." In a very brief introduction, the editors call Lutie a "fictional rendering of the Negro Matriarchy." They encourage comparisons between Petry's matriarch and the sociological description of the matriarch by sociologist Kenneth Clark.

151 Dempsey, David. "Uncle Tom's Ghost and the Literary Abolitionists." *Antioch Review* 6, no. 3 (Fall 1946): 442–447.

Gives Petry credit for displacing exclusive African-American "types" in literature like "Uncle Tom," "poverty-stricken Willie," and "happy-go-lucky Josh." Applauds her for creating professionals and government workers with "much deserved intelligence, dignity, and courage." Does, however, indict Petry for the murder scene in *The Street*, claiming it lacks "poetic justice."

152 Downing, Francis. *Commonweal* 47 (2 January 1948): 306–307.

Takes issue with one critic who reviewed *Country Place* as "real [and] most compelling." To the contrary, says Petry is "not clear" and is not a "born story-teller." Approves, however, of Petry's naming the unfaithful wife of the main character Glory, concluding that through Glory's symbolic name Petry is saying that "what ruins our marriage is the adolescent and romantic process of falling in love."

153 Doyle, Sister Mary Ellen. "The Heroine in Black Novels." In *Perspectives on Afro-American Women*. Edited by Willa D. Johnson and Thomas L. Green. Washington, DC: ECCA (Divison of Educational-Community Counselors Associates, Inc.), 1975.

Includes Lutie Johnson from *The Street* in her analysis of black heroines in African-American fiction. Says Petry joins a host of other black women writers who raise issues that are crucial to gender and race. Is not convinced, however, that Lutie's unsuccessful fight for security and respectability is "fully . . . tragedy."

154 Eisenger, Chester E. *Fiction of the Forties*. Chicago: University of Chicago Press, 1963.

Introduces *The Street* along with other new works by African-American writers from the 1940s. Calls Petry's novel "tightly plotted."

155 Emanuel, James. Ann Petry. In *Contemporary Novelists*. Edited by D. L. Kirkpatrick. London: St. James, 1972. Reprint. 1986.

Provides terse critiques of all three of Petry's novels. Calls *The Street* more than just another example of environmental determinism overshadowed by its precursor, *Native Son*. Says *Country Place* is another of Petry's attacks "against a cash-and-carry society hostile to moral beauty." Concludes that *The Narrows* is a novel "about love and its betrayal." Insists Petry's "craftsmanship, social truth, and humanity . . . deserve wider recognition."

156 ———. Ann Petry. In *Contemporary Novelists*. Edited by James Vinson. 2d Edition. New York: St. Martin's, 1976.

Analysis of Petry's first three novels, suggesting that the endings in *The Street* and *Country Place* are marred from the beginning by their seemingly "conjured " theses. Calls for wider recognition, however, of Petry's craftsmanship and humanity.

157 Emanuel, James A., and Theodore L. Gross. Introduction. *Dark Symphony: Negro in Literature in America.* New York: Free Press, 1968.

Mentions Petry's second and third novels, seeing *Country Place,* with its metaphors and symbols, as reminiscent of Hawthorne, and calling *The Narrows* a modification of the basically sociological approach taken with the family's environment in *The Street.*

158 "Emotional Impact in Novel on Slum-Shocked Negroes." Review of *The Street. Weekly People,* 13 April 1946 [Special Collections, Boston University].

Provides a Marxist critique of *The Street.* Says the "enlightened and class conscious worker . . . who can give his aroused emotions directions" can benefit from Petry's "emotional-arousing novel."

159 Engle, Paul. "Heroine Keeps Her Integrity in Cruel Street." *Chicago Tribune,* 10 February 1946, 12.

Writes that *The Street,* with its realizations about the "actual forces of race and environment," is "stronger than any argument about the Negro." Concludes that the novel is proof that "Negroes" are equally human.

160 Ervin, Hazel Arnett. "Just a Few Questions More, Mrs. Petry." Philadelphia, PA, 1989. [See p. 101, this volume.]

Posed to the writer are questions left unanswered in other interviews and critiques. [See full interview in this bibliography.]

161 ———. "The Subversion of Cultural Ideology in Ann Petry's *The Street* and *Country Place.*" Ph.D. diss., Howard University, 1993.

Coded in specific chapters in *The Street* and *Country Place* is Petry's discontent with patriarchal ideology concerning the woman's place. From these chapters, among the women characters, there also emerges a sense of feminine consciousness.

162 Fein, Esther B. "An Author's Look at 1940's Harlem Is Being Reissued." *New York Times,* 8 January 1992, C13.

Compares Petry's "street" in 1946 to today's "street," concluding conditions are no better. Reviews Petry's rise to "sudden fame" with the publication of *The Street* and her sudden departure from Harlem to New England's Old Saybrook. Photographs from 1946 and 1992 are provided.

163 Feld, Rose. "Tragedy on Two Levels,' *New York Herald Tribune Weekly Book Review,* 5 October 1947, 6.

Reviews *Country Place* briefly. Says Petry's motif of the returning soldier who discovers his wife has been unfaithful is one that is popular among novelists during the forties. Thinks *Country Place* is "exceedingly good," primarily because of the "feel of a small town, the integrity of dialogue, and the portrayal of Johnnie, Glory, [and] Mrs. Gramby." Concludes, however, that the novel has its flaw: Petry changes from first- to third-person narrator.

164 "First Novel." *Ebony* (April 1946): 35–39.

Gives an account of the cocktail party sponsored by the editors at Houghton Mifflin at New York's Biltmore Hotel in honor of Petry and her successful first novel, *The Street.* Included are pictures of Petry with notable critics, writers, and stage and screen celebrities. Includes biographical information.

165 Fisher, Dexter, ed. "Contexts and Narratives." In *The Third Woman.* Boston: Houghton Mifflin, 1980.

Contends that Petry's "Doby's Gone" helps to explain the "complexity of black female sensibility" by "magnifying the realities" of discrimination for even a black female child.

166 Ford, Nick Aaron. "A Blueprint for Negro Authors." *Phylon* 11, no. 4 (Fourth Quarter 1950): 374–377. Reprint. *Black Expressions.* Edited by Addison Gayle, Jr. New York: Weybright and Talley, 1969.

Suggests a blueprint for writers "who wish to accept the glorious opportunities and grave responsibilities of the next half century." Praises Petry for having demonstrated a mastery of craftsmanship and design in *The Street,* but criticizes her for abandoning racial themes in *Country Place* in favor of universal themes. Says *Country Place* is greatly inferior to *The Street.*

167 ———. "From Test Tube to Typewriter." *Afro-American* (Baltimore), 11 December 1948, 3.

Traces Petry's career from pharmacist to novelist. Compares the writer with other "first" American women writers of literature—both black and white. Offers quotes by Petry on the role of the African-American writer.

168 "Fortitude Sustains Movement." *Hartford Courant,* 2 March 1986, A14.

Outlines Petry's writing habits. Provides a very brief discussion of Petry's "first born"—*The Street.* Identifies the women in Petry's family who contributed to her success.

169 "From Pestle to Pen." *Headlines and Pictures* (March 1946): 42–43.

Features an essay/interview with Petry as well as a review of *The Street.* Notes that in the novel, there are repeated testimonies of the hazards of single mothers raising children in "an environment of squalor and viciousness." In response to these repeated images in her work, Petry is quoted as saying that "women's problems have been [her] longtime interests." She shares how she learned from observations when she lived in

Harlem the "problems of mothers leaving children [alone while they went] to work." The children "paid the price." The reviewer concludes that *The Street* is at its best when it is "pleading the cause of Negro women and children" and at its weakest when "its characters become enlarged in a melodramatic series of events."

170   Fuller, Edmund. "'Unbelievable' Is Word for It." *Chicago Sunday Tribune,* 23 August 1953, 5.
      Gives a remorseful yet unfavorable review of *The Narrows,* calling it a "lurid . . . sensational . . . and sympathetic story." Finds the "tragic love" motif unbelievable. Calls Link and Camilo "demoralized persons, in their different ways."

171   Fuller, Hoyt W. "Contemporary Negro Fiction." In *The Black American Writer. Vol. 1: Fiction.* Edited by C. W. E. Bigsby. Deland, FL: Everett/ Edwards, 1969.
      Writes that "the contemporary Negro novelist and playwright [are] heirs of Richard Wright." Briefly looking at other excellent novelists who write in the wake of Wright, Fuller includes Petry. He calls her "the most promising novelist" and "a superb but uneven literary craftsman."

172   Fuller, James E. "Harlem Portrait." *Pittsburgh Courier,* 9 February 1946 [Special Collections, Boston University].
      Offers personal impressions of Petry: "serious but charming" and "Harlem's adopted daughter." Quotes Petry's reasons for writing *The Street.*

173   Gannett, Lewis. Review of *The Street. New York Herald Tribune Book Review,* 7 February 1946, 21.
      Writes that while Petry's novel is swift and absorbing, its melodramatic ending is objectionable. Believes readers deserve solutions to the economic and racial problems that are so convincingly raised in *The Street.*

174   Garrett, Lula Jones. *Afro-American* (Baltimore), 13 September 1958, 13.
      States briefly that Petry is the "first woman scriptwriter on the West Coast" to be employed by Columbia Pictures. Calls her a journeyman for the screenplay *That Hill Girl.*

175   Gayle, Addison, Jr. "Perhaps Not So Soon One Morning." *Phylon* 26, no. 4 (Winter 1968): 397.
      Refutes Hill, who suggests in *Soon One Morning* that James Baldwin and Ralph Ellison are the most capable forerunners of African-American writers entering the "mainstream" of American literature. Gayle insists

that Baldwin's Ida Scott has been drawn more artistically by Petry in *The Street.*

176 ———. *The Way of the New World: The Black Novel in America.* Garden City, NY: Anchor/Doubleday, 1975.

Defines Lutie in *The Street* as one of the "Black Rebel[s]" who follow Bigger Thomas in *Native Son,* but warns that *The Street* is not a carbon copy of *Native Son.* Rather, the novel is "a powerful and provocative work exploring areas that Wright, taking his reader for granted, did not venture to explore." Too, the novel "moves" beyond the social Darwinists, insisting upon salvation of its people along classical lines: "change the society and there will be no Juntos, Boots Smiths, Mins, or Joneses." Furthermore, Gayle says the novel takes on "dimensions of a mock-heroic epic."

177 Gelfant, Blanche Housman. *The American City Novel.* Norman: University of Oklahoma Press, 1954. Reprint. 1970.

Discusses the city novel as a literary genre and concludes that three forms of the city novel exist: the "portrait" study, the "synoptic" study, and the "ecological" study. Names works by Theodore Dreiser, John Dos Passos, and James T. Farrell to support thesis. Briefly mentions Petry's *The Street* as an example of the "ecological" novel.

178 "General Courses." In *All the Women Are White, All the Blacks Are Men, But Some of Us Are Brave.* Edited by Gloria T. Hull, Patricia Bell Scott, and Barbara Smith. Old Westbury, NY: Feminist Press, 1982.

A network of general topics, genres, and critical sources for teaching black women writers. Also included are course outlines by Barbara Smith, Gloria T. Hull, Theresa R. Love, and Alice Walker as well as Fahamisha Shariat's "Blakwomen Writers of the U.S.A. Who Are They, What Do They Write?" Short stories and novels by Petry are recommended.

179 Giddings, Paula. Review of *The Street. Essence* (March 1989): 36.

Calls Lutie's story one "with a message." Classifies Petry's novel as an "exciting mystery-murder thriller." Encourages a rereading.

180 Gilbert, Sandra M., and Susan Gubar. "Fighting for Life." In *No Man's Land: Vol. 1, The War of the Words.* New Haven: Yale University Press, 1988.

Questions whether "late nineteenth- and twentieth-century literary women transform[ed] their words into weapons in order to wrest authority from [literary] men." Concludes that the "text . . . in the black tradition has enable[d] female artists to translate the comparatively subtle terms of sexual struggle into the more openly theatrical terms of . . . racial struggle." Further concludes that Petry's *The Street* is a "documentary text representing the battle of the sexes not only as a racial but also as a class struggle."

181 Girson, Rochelle. "Ann Petry Sets Novel in Home Town, Saybrook." *Hartford Times,* 15 August 1953 [Special Collections, Boston University].

Reveals that *The Narrows* is set in Old Saybrook, Connecticut. Moreover, quotes Petry's responses to those who object to the interracial love affair between Link and Camilo and to those who call the novel propaganda. Also includes personal anecdotes by Petry on writing fiction.

182 Gloster, Hugh M. "Race and the Negro Writer." *Phylon* 11, no. 4 (Fourth Quarter 1950): 369–373. Reprint. *Black Expressions.* Edited by Addison Gayle, Jr. New York: Weybright and Talley, 1969.

Writes that continued use of racial subjects has handicapped "Negro" writers by lessening their "cosmic grasp of varied experience, philosophical perspective, literary range, contributions to cultural integration." Explains, however, how Petry is an exception.

183 Goldsmith, Alfred. "Struggle for Survival." *New Masses* 59 (21 May 1946): 25–26.

Reviews *The Street.* Contends Petry's characters are only "sketchy outlines of human beings."

184 Goodwin, Polly. "Kitten with Temper Short as His Tail." *Chicago Sunday Tribune,* Part 4, 13 November 1949, 6.

Takes title from a passage in the story *The Drugstore Cat,* which in essence captures the complications in Buzzie's existence. Calls the book "a little gem . . . for children."

185 Green, Marjorie. "Ann Petry Planned to Write." *Opportunity: Journal of Negro Life* 24, no. 2 (April–June 1946): 78–79.

Provides a mini-portrait of Petry as the artist, starting with her high school graduation and ending with her Houghton Mifflin Fellowship Award.

186 Gregory, John. "Ann Petry Writes about a Negro Girl's Problems." *New York Sun,* 7 February 1946, 21.

Says Petry puts to "good use" her firsthand knowledge of Harlem and its problems, even the black man's inhumanity to other blacks. Applauds the writer for her natural intrusions to address the "Negro problem" and for her avoidance of "pseudo-literary" effects.

187 Gross, Theodore L. "Ann Petry: The Novelist as Social Critic." In *Black Fiction: New Studies in the Afro-American Novel since 1945.* Edited by A. Robert Lee. New York: Barnes and Noble, 1980.

Quoting Petry and several of her works, Gross provides support for the following concepts: Petry "has the heart of a naturalist and the head of a realist"; the novel is for Petry "an instrument of social criticism"; and in all of Petry's short stories, the leitmotif is "racial identity."

188 Gustafson, Lucy. "Old Saybrook Author Will Speak on Witchcraft at Meeting Jan. 23." *New Era,* 15 January 1970, 8.

Announces that Petry will be guest speaker at a membership meeting of the Old Saybrook Historical Society. Offers quotes from Petry explaining how she was influenced to write *Tituba of Salem Village.*

189 "Harlem." In *Encyclopedia of Black America.* Edited by W. Augustus Low. New York: McGraw-Hill, 1981.

Describes Harlem in terms of its geography. Mentions Petry's *The Street* along with Claude Brown's *Manchild in the Promised Land* as novels that reveal the role Harlem streets play in the lives of African-American residents.

190 "Harlem Made Ann Petry Write Her Novel." *PM* (3 March 1946): M4.

Shows that Petry personally observed "the kinds of violence" she wrote about. For instance, as a local newspaperwoman, Petry covered a story about the owner of a delicatessen stabbing an African-American youth in the back. The youth staggered out of the store and collapsed on the sidewalk. This same incident appears in *The Street.*

191 Harris, Trudier. "On Southern and Northern Maids: Geography, Mammies, and Militants." In *From Mammies to Militants: Domestics in Black American Literature.* Philadelphia: Temple University Press, 1982.

Says Lutie in *The Street* typifies the "transitional" or "moderate" northern maid in literature. Like the folkloric Br'er Rabbit or Staggolie, Lutie, aware of her history and culture, makes "no pretense about who she is or what she thinks." According to Harris, Lutie insists on recognition of her "humanity." Unlike the southern maid Mammy Jane in Charles Chesnutt's *Marrow of Tradition,* Lutie "sees her job as a means to an end, not as an end in itself."

192 Harrison, William. Review of *The Street. Boston Chronicle.* 23 February 1946 [Special Collections, Boston University].

Describes Petry as the "most profound contemporary Negro novelist specializing in sociological fiction." Calls her novel persuasive yet imaginative argumentation. Compares the story's "action"—action that moves without deviation to its conclusion—to the action of a Greek tragedy by Sophocles or Euripides.

193 Hernton, Calvin. "The Significance of Ann Petry." In *The Sexual Mountain and Black Women Writers, Adventures in Sex, Literature, and Real Life.* New York: Anchor/Doubelday, 1987. Reprint. 1990. Also appears in *Wild Women in the Whirlwind.* Edited by Joanne M. Braxton and Andree Nicola McLaughlin. New Brunswick, NJ: Rutgers University Press, 1990.

Concludes that *The Street* "is the first work of social realism and naturalism written from an all but complete Womanist Perspective."

Says that "No one until Petry, male or female, had so thoroughly portrayed black women as victims of Multiple Oppression (economic, racial, and sexual), and no one had so boldly portrayed black men as the levelers of a significant measure of that oppression." Hernton compares and contrasts the "fear" of Bigger Thomas with the "rage" of Lutie Johnson.

194   Hill, Herbert, ed. Introduction. *Soon One Morning: New Writing by American Negroes 1940–1962.* New York: Knopf, 1965. Reprint. 1968.
      Displays a diversity of contemporary writings by African-Americans, including Petry's "Miss Muriel." In his introduction, Hill places Petry among writers who "joined the tradition of social protest" when she wrote *The Street.* He concludes that *Country Place* "foreshadows" future novels that will deal with nonblack characters and issues.

195   Hill-Lubin, Mildred A. "African Religion: That Invisible Institution in African and African-American Literature." In *Interdisciplinary Dimensions of African Literature.* Edited by Kofi Anyidoho, Abioseh M. Porter, Daniel Racine, and Janice Spleth. Washington, DC: Three Continents, 1985.
      Discusses the ambiguities in Petry's characters Min and Jones (*The Street*), particularly in regard to the influences of religion and magic in their lives.

196   Hinterberg, Helen J. "Helping Teens Be Literate in History." *Christian Science Monitor,* 28 March 1989, 14.
      Suggests that Petry allows the reader "to see and feel the historical realities that helped create" *Tituba of Salem Village.*

197   ———. Review of *Harriet Tubman, Conductor on the Underground Railroad. Christian Science Monitor,* 8 September 1989, 13.
      Recommends *Harriet Tubman* for avid young readers who want books that are "structured with episode[s]" or that tell "what really happened."

198   Hobson, Laura Z. Review of *The Narrows. Saturday Review of Literature* (15 August 1953): 6.
      Announces the release of *The Narrows* by Houghton Mifflin. Admits to know no more than what appears on the publisher's release: "a love story" that took "five years" to write.

199   Holzman, Robert. Review of *Harriet Tubman, Conductor on the Underground Railroad. Kirkus* 23 (1 June 1955): 366.
      Details the biography as being "poignant and sensitive reality," especially when compared with other such attempts by other writers.

200 Houck, Anne Cleaver. "Plot Keyed to Social Taboo Lacks Punch." *Gazette* (Little Rock), 23 August 1953 [Special Collections, Boston University].

Contends that while *The Narrows* reveals "errors in our civilization," its projection of an "affaire de coeur between an educated Negro and a wanton young matron of the haut monde" lacks realism.

201 "Houghton Mifflin Awards Tenth Annual Fellowships." *Publishers' Weekly* (March 1945): 1202.

Identifies Petry as the recipient of the tenth annual Houghton Mifflin Literary Fellowship Award in fiction; says she received $2,400.

202 Hughes, Carl Milton. "Common Denominator: Man." In *The Negro Novelist: 1940–1950, A Discussion of the Writings of American Negro Novelists 1940–1950*. New York: Citadel, 1953. Reprint. 1970.

Maintains that Petry exhibits "a high level of competence in fictional writing" in *Country Place*. Discusses the novel's influences such as Sinclair Lewis's *Main Street*, Victorian standards of high moral conduct and strict decorum, and Dickensian creations. Focuses on plot, characterization, and language in the novel. Finds fault with the novel's shift from narrator to characters, calling the technique "cumbersome."

203 ———. "Portrayals of Bitterness." In *The Negro Novelist: 1940–1950, A Discussion of the Writings of American Negro Novelists 1940–1950*. New York: Citadel, 1953. Reprint. 1970.

First book-length critical analysis of *The Street*. Focuses on characterization, setting, point of view, and plot. Hughes is convinced that Petry's thesis is naturalistic but calls her techniques refreshing and advanced, especially in comparison with contemporaries like Wright (*Native Son*) and Fannie Cook (*Mrs. Palmer's Honey*). Concludes that Lutie is a "tragic figure" in a "modern tragedy."

204 Ingram, Elwarda Deloris. "Black Women: Literary Self-Portraits." *DAI* 41 (1980): 3573A. University of Oregon.

Contends that "black women characters, as presented in the literature of some black male writers and white writers, have often been portrayed as one-dimensional figures: the patient, the long-suffering servant, the matriarch, the religious fanatic, and the nigger wench." Seeks to prove that "black women writers have created black women characters who are full-dimensional and more realistically drawn than other writers have done." Petry's Lutie of *The Street* is one example of a more realistically drawn black female character.

205 ———. "The Suspended Black Woman in Literature." *MAWA Review* 1, no. 1 (Spring 1982): 20–23.

Defining the suspended woman as one who is powerless and unfulfilled, leading a life of blind or numb existence, Ingram examines four black characters as suspended women: Nanny in *Their Eyes Were Watching God,* Mariah in *This Child's Gonna Live,* Sula in *Sula,* and Lutie in *The Street.*

206 "Ill Home Life as Worse than Lynching." *Afro-American* (Baltimore), 30 March 1946 [Special Collections, Boston University].

Reiterates Petry's reasons for writing *The Street*: "to show why colored people [have] a high crime rate, a high death rate, and little or no chance of keeping [their families] intact in large Northern cities."

207 Issacs, Diana Scharfeld. "Ann Petry's Life and Art: Piercing Stereotypes." *DAI* 43 (1982): 446A. Columbia University Teachers College.

Provides a critical look at Petry's life and art, acknowledging her particular contributions to African-American literature and to American literature overall.

208 Ivey, James. "Ann Petry Talks about First Novel." *Crisis* 53, no. 2 (February 1946): 48–49. Also appears in *Sturdy Black Bridges: Visions of Black Women in Literature.* Edited by Roseann P. Bell, Bettye J. Parker, and Beverly Guy-Sheftall. Garden City, NY: Anchor/Doubleday, 1979, and this volume, p. 69.

Introduces Petry as a new artist. Quotes the writer on why she wrote *The Street.* [See full interview this bibliography.]

209 ———. "Mrs. Petry's Harlem." *Crisis* 53, no. 5 (May 1946): 154–155.

Renders an unfavorable review of *The Street.* Questions Petry's "living portrait of Harlem"—the street. Says the writer fails to depict "normal and responsible people in the [African-American] community." Argues that Lutie's failures are not directly related to "the street" or to bigotry. Rather, Lutie inevitably fails because of her naivete and poor choice of male friends.

210 Izard, Anne. Review of *Tituba of Salem Village. Grade Teacher* (February 1965): 29.

Considers the story about a West Indian woman who is tried as a witch in Salem to be a vivid presentation. Attributes the success of the work to Petry's "controlled" style.

211 Jackson, Blyden. "A Review of J. L. Dillard's 'Black English.'" *Journal of Negro History* 58, no. 1 (January 1973): 90–96. Reprint. *The Waiting Years.* Edited by Blyden Jackson. Baton Rouge: Louisiana State University Press, 1976. Reprint. 1977.

Uses his own "ready references" and the "speech patterns" of ordinary black characters in fiction to rebuke aspects of Dillard's study of Pidgin English. Identifies Petry as an exemplary creator of such black characters.

212 ———. "A Survey Course in Negro Literature." *College English* 35 (March 1973): 631–636. Reprint. *The Waiting Years.* Edited by Blyden Jackson. Baton Rouge: Louisiana State University Press, 1976.

Advocates a required comprehensive general course in African-American literature at the college level. Calls for the inclusion of an "Age of Wright," or a "golden age" because writers from the 1940s like Petry present the "Negro, new or old, as he actually [is]."

213 ———. "An Essay in Criticism." *Phylon* 11, no. 4 (Fourth Quarter 1950): 338–343. Reprint. *The Waiting Years.* Edited by Blyden Jackson. Baton Rouge: Louisiana State University Press, 1966. Reprint. 1976.

Calls for "the development of an energetic scholarly criticism" from African-American critics—a criticism that will also be an "integrative factor" in America. Encourages critics to "reflect upon the life-giving quality of Ann Petry's imagination in *The Street.*"

214 Jackson, Blyden. "Of Irony in Negro Fiction: A Critical Study." Ph.D. diss., University of Michigan, 1952.

Earliest dissertation on Petry (the only available copy is located in the Petry Collection in the African-American Center at Shaw University). Provides a working definition of irony, then suggests that because irony is a continuum in the American society, African-American artists have difficulty being satirists or ironists. Thinks, however, that Petry in *The Street* and Gardner Smith in *Last of the Conquerors* are more successful than Jessie Fauset in *Comedy, American Style* and Walter White in *The Fire in the Flint.*

215 ———. "The Ghetto of the Negro Novel: A Theme with Variations." *NCTE* [from the Discovery of English: NCTE 1971 *Distinguished Lectures.* Urbana, IL: National Council of Teachers of English]. Reprint. *The Waiting Years.* Edited by Blyden Jackson. Baton Rouge: Louisiana State University Press, 1976.

Writes that the "ghetto of the Negro novel has served the Negro novelist as an objective correlative for his disdain of the pretentions of color caste." Discusses novelists' variations of the ghetto—Petry's included. Insists that "Negro" novelists have had one distinguishable "common voice" when addressing such a theme.

216 ———. "The Negro's Image of His Universe as Reflected in His Fiction." *CLA Journal* 4, no. 1 (September 1960): 22–31. Reprint. *Images of the Negro in America.* Edited by Darwin T. Turner and Jean M. Bright. Boston: D. C. Heath, 1965. Reprint. *The Waiting Years.* Edited by Blyden Jackson. Baton Rouge: Louisiana State University Press, 1976.

Suggests there are "distinctive" characteristics in the universe of "Negro fiction": a ghetto and a nonghetto, irony that causes pleasure and pain, and a static world. Uses Petry's *The Street* and *Country Place* to help support this thesis.

217 ———. "The Negro's Negro in Negro Literature." *Michigan Quarterly Review* 4, no. 4 (October 1965): 290–295.

Points to *The Street* and *The Narrows* as "changing reflection[s] of discontent." Provides a literary history of the "dominant character" in black fiction, suggesting that Lutie in *The Street* is like her contemporaries in *Native Son, If He Hollers Let Him Go,* and *Last of the Conquerors*—that is, she is "embittered and brutalized by the experience of life forced upon [her] by America"; or, she is "full to bursting of pent-up violence and venom." Jackson concludes that the "dominant character" in black fiction changes with the main character in *Invisible Man* and with Link Williams in *The Narrows*—each character "withdraw[s]" and "search[es] for [his] identity."

218 ———. *The Waiting Years*. Baton Rouge: Louisiana State University Press, 1966. Reprint. 1976.

Includes a number of essays that give his critical attention to Petry. (See Nos. 211, 212, 213, 215, 216 this volume.)

219 Jackson, Clara O. Ann Petry. In *Twentieth Century Children's Writers*. Edited by D. L. Kirkpatrick. London: Macmillan, 1978. Reprint. 1983.

Reviews Petry's three juvenile works, noting how each involves research by the author. Also provides plot summaries. Praises Petry's deep-seated interest in adding to both the "accuracy and adequacy of ... history."

220 James, Charles L., ed. *From the Roots: Short Stories by Black Americans*. New York: Dodd, Mead, 1970.

Concludes that Petry is "sensitive and aware" of role reversals in the African-American community after World War II. Reprints short story "Like A Winding Sheet." Following the story, there are questions that deal with the story's construction and its social significance.

221 Jarrett, Thomas D. "Recent Fiction by Negroes." *College English* 16, no. 2 (November 1954): 85–91.

Notes how *Native Son* marks the appearance of a "new kind" of fiction by "Negroes"—that is, a literature that represents realistically aspects of the "Negro" experiences, a literature that has universal appeal and relevance. Points to Petry who Jarrett says "reflect[s] the nature of new materials and techniques." For instance, concludes that notwithstanding her sermonizing in *The Street,* Petry has "undeniable universal appeal." Says her 116th Street can be compared with the heath in Hardy's *Return of the Native.* Jarrett considers *The Street* a "masterpiece of its kind," even though it is at times "clumsy." He merely mentions

Country Place, calling it one example where black writers write about nonblack characters.

222 ———. "Toward Unfettered Creativity: A Note on the Negro Novelist's Coming of Age." *Phylon* 11, no. 4 (Fourth Quarter 1950): 313–317.

Notes that much has been said about the "Negro novelist having come of age" rather than about what is still required of him before he can attain "maturity in the realm of fiction writing." Jarrett suggests "a growing social consciousness and a universality in the treatment of themes," a "higher regard for literary values," and a "catholicity in treatment of themes." Cites Petry for having achieved most of these objectives.

223 Jaskoski, Helen. "Power Unequal to Man: The Significance of Conjure in Works by Five Afro-American Authors." *Southern Folklore Quarterly* 38, no. 2 (June 1974): 81–108.

Examines the significance of "conjure" in *The Street.* Concludes Petry depicts a less ambiguous practice of the root doctor as a means to solve problems (for Min), and that Min's decision to seek the root doctor is her first attempt to take control of her own life.

224 Johns, Robert L. Ann Petry. In *Notable Black American Women.* Edited by Jessie Carney Smith. Detroit: Gale Research, 1992.

Discusses thematic makeup of Petry's novels as well as Petry's philosophy as a writer. An incorrect year of birth given. References of Petry's criticism range from the 1940s to the 1980s.

225 Joyce, Joyce Ann. Ann Petry. *Nethula Journal* 2 (1982): 16–20.

Contends that the African-American and American literary communities have failed to trust the donnée in Ann Petry's works. Thus, Petry has drifted somewhat into obscurity. Joyce offers ways in which one might approach Petry's novels and still respect what and how Petry has chosen to write. For example, she makes a lengthy comparison between Ellison's Invisible Man and Petry's Link Williams from *The Narrows*—two men who struggle from early adolescence to come to terms with their relationships to white society.

226 Kaiser, Ernest. "The Literature of Harlem." *Freedomways* 3, no. 3 (Summer 1963): 276–291. Reprint. *Black Expressions.* Edited by Gayle Addison, Jr. New York: Waybright and Tally, 1969.

Correlates sociological and literary materials that make up a chronological overview of Harlem. Mentions in the section "Literature of the War Years" that Petry's *The Street* is "an honest attempt to sum up what the author saw and heard." In the section "Other Writers about Harlem," Kaiser discusses Petry's article "Harlem" in *Holiday,* calling the article a "kind of cooks' [*sic*] tour" of Harlem with some interpretations displayed with pictures—"beautiful . . . [and] in rich colors."

227 Kamme-Erkel, Sybille. *Happily Ever After?: Marriage and Its Rejection in Afro-American Novels.* New York: Peter Lang, 1989.

Exploring the rejection of marriage in African-American novels, primarily written by women, Kamme-Erkel looks at causes for "breakdowns." Using Petry's *The Street,* the writer concludes that in this novel, marriage between Lutie and Jim breaks down "solely because of economic problems."

228 Kazin, Alfred. "Brothers Crying Out for More Access to Life." *Saturday Review,* 2 October 1971, 33–35.

Compares Petry with the young "race" writers from the 1960s, explaining how Petry's *Miss Muriel and Other Stories* is "different" and "slow" in "rhythm." Praises Petry's efforts, however, particularly her artistry in "Miss Muriel."

229 Kent, George E. "Struggle for the Image: Selected Books by or about Blacks during 1971." *Phylon* 33, no. 4 (Winter 1972): 304–311.

Surveys books that are recovering, consolidating, or intensifying black images for greater understanding. Includes *Miss Muriel and Other Stories,* citing Petry as highly competent with her shorter fiction.

230 Kiken, Jonas. "Love under an Evil Star." *Post* (Denver), 13 September 1953 [Special Collections, Boston University].

Cites Petry among a number of African-American writers who once lived among the people in her novels. When reviewing *The Narrows,* Kiken calls attention to plot and characters, particularly the editor of the local newspaper, Pete Bullock, who strongly resembles Sinclair Lewis's "targets of the ulcerated strivers" and to Mamie Powther (Petry's depiction of "the earthy side" of women).

231 L'Engle, Madeleine. Review of *Tituba of Salem Village. New York Times Book Review.* Section 7, Part II, 1 November 1964, 8.

Says work goes beyond the historical accounts of Tituba and deals with universal issues like race and Christianity. Calls the book a tribute to Petry's "artistry."

232 Lattin, Vernon E. "Ann Petry and the American Dream." *Black American Literature Forum* 12, no. 2 (Summer 1978): 69–72.

Urges rereadings and reevaluations of all of Petry's works. Says critics fail to see Petry as a "rebel." Lattin forcefully contends that Petry is a "significant critic of American values" in all three of her novels.

233 Lebow, Diane. "Selfhood in Free Fall: Novels by Black and White American Women." *DAI* 46 (1985): 3034A. University of California, Santa Cruz.

Writes that novels by African-American women and novels by white American women suggest a "new development of the *Bildungsroman* tradition in that the female character who evolves a stronger sense of self seems to be existing from a culture which appears less and less likely to assimilate her." Furthermore, this new development of the *Bildungsroman* is a "casting off of old traditional patterns of being a woman in order to formulate new ones," or a "free fall."

234 Lenz, Gunter H. "Symbolic Space, Communal Rituals, and the Surreality of the Urban Ghetto: Harlem in Black Literature from the 1920s to the 1960s." *Callaloo* 2, no. 2 (Spring 1988): 332–335.

Discusses the "literary strategies" or "patterns" used by African-American writers in their responses to the transformation of Harlem from "Negro capital" of the 1920s to "ghetto . . . of the 1950s and 1960s." Concludes that Petry, when "dramatizing the tensions between social structure and communities in *The Street* . . . poses the question of whether there [is] any meaning and strength left at all in black writers' cherished and stubborn dream of Harlem as the place and incorporation of black urban culture and community."

235 Littlejohn, David. Introduction. *Black on White: A Critical Survey of Writing by American Negroes.* New York: Viking, 1966.

Makes special pleas in his introduction and in chapter seven for Petry to be reviewed as a "careful, wise and sympathetic" writer. Considers Petry's style masculine, crisp, and energetic with threads of irony, but thinks "out of the female wisdom, she creates her characters." Says, like Victorians, she creates "sordid plots." Calls Petry's details of Harlem "convincingly complete," but considers *The Street* quasi-protest literature.

236 Locke, Alain. "A Critical Retrospect of the Literature of the Negro for 1947." *Phylon* 9, no. 1 (First Quarter 1948): 7.

Looks back over the literature by African-American writers in 1947. Says Petry's *Country Place* "has neither the surge nor the social significance of her first novel."

237 ———. "Reason and Race: A Review of the Literature of the Negro for 1946." *Phylon* 8, no. 1 (First Quarter 1947): 17, 21.

Includes *The Street* in his review of a host of books written by African-American writers in 1946. Hails *The Street* as the "artistic success of the year." Also calls the work "quiet, courageous, unsentimental realism." Disagrees with critics who call the novel's ending defeatist. Rather, he says the work is the "cleverest kind of social indictment—Zolaesque."

238 "Lost Persons in Love." *Nation* 177 (29 August 1953): 177.

Criticizes the structure and style in *The Narrows,* citing both as being too varied in one work. Concludes, however, that Petry means well with her "violent and passionate" story about two lost souls.

239 M. C. R. "An Eloquent Statement of a Racial Problem found in Harlem's Streets." *Sunday Star* (Washington, DC), 10 February 1946, 3.

Applauds Petry for not idealizing her characters. Thinks Petry, like Shakespeare, presents characters with feelings. However, disagrees with Petry's viewpoint that Lutie's situation is limited only to young black women. Also disagrees with Petry's "too-violent climax" in the novel.

240 M. P. "Evil Results of Crowding." *Worcester Telegram,* 10 February 1946, [Special Collections, Boston University].

Insists that in *The Street,* Petry is angry with "an attitude of mind and with the conditions which breed immorality and crime.'

241 M. P. "Sordid Side of Town Life." *Worcester Sunday Telegram,* 28 September 1947 [Special Collections, Boston University].

Compares Petry's second novel with her first. Says both "are powerfully written and [that] their characters haunt one." Concludes, however, that neither presents "a pretty picture of life." Due to what he calls a flaw in the narration, the reviewer urges Petry to write another book—"wholly from the druggist's view."

242 M. W. "The Latest Negro Novel." *Christian Science Monitor,* 8 February 1946, 14.

Calls *The Street* "ugly and revolting in the extreme." Questions why Petry as an African-American woman would write such a violent treatment of Harlem life and give the impression that overall Harlem is "deplorable."

243 MacCann, Donnarae. "Black Americans." *Christian Science Monitor,* 1 May 1969, B7.

Calls *Harriet Tubman, Conductor on the Underground Railroad* and *Tituba of Salem Village* distinguished biographies that for a change are "from a Black American's viewpoint."

244 McCarthy, Dorsey. "'The Street' Effective Weapon on Racial Bigotry." *Chicago Bee,* 17 March 1946, 16.

Thinks there is a race between Lutie and "the street" for the possession of Bub. Praises Petry for her depictions of unforgettable persons rather than types. Calls on every woman's club in America to review *The Street.*

245 McDowell, Margaret B. "'The Narrows': A Fuller View of Ann Petry." *Black American Literature Forum* 14, no. 4 (Winter 1980): 135–141.

Provides an extensive critical assessment of Petry's third novel within three fully developed themes: "the oppressiveness of guilt; the effects of historiography, tradition, and time on the attitudes of contemporary people toward race; and the limited veracity of sensory apprehension." Looks specifically at such techniques as flashback and symbolism, and such elements as point of view and characterization.

246 McGuire, A. B. Review of *Harriet Tubman, Conductor on the Underground Railroad. New York Herald Tribune Book Review,* 13 November 1955, Section 6, Part II, 8.
Applauds the biography and says it is vividly focused and convincingly well written.

247 McKay, Nellie. Introduction. *The Narrows.* Boston: Beacon, 1988.
Provides a lengthy critique of Petry's "creative vision" in *The Street* and *Country Place.* Concludes that the writer sharpens her creative vision in *The Narrows.* Calls attention to this work for its "complex and entangled relationships with demonstrable implications for contemporary feminist criticism." (See Number 313 for criticism on the Introduction.)

248 ———. "Reflections on Black Women Writers: Revising the Literary Canon." *The Impact of Feminist Research in the Academy.* Edited by Christie Farnham. Bloomington: Indiana University Press, 1987.
Concludes that "what black women as writers have consistently provided for themselves and others has been a rendering of the black woman's place in the world in which she lives, as she shapes and defines that from her own impulses and actions." Considers Petry as one of those women. Discusses briefly Petry's *The Street.*

249 McSherry, Elizabeth. "Moses of Her People." *Hartford Courant,* 14 August 1955, 19.
Reviews *Harriet Tubman, Conductor on the Underground Railroad* at length. Provides a plot summary and characterizes Petry's portrayal of Tubman as "vital and magnetic." Predicts that students in American history will profit from Petry's biography.

250 Madden, David. "Ann Petry: 'The Witness.'" *Studies in Black Literature* 6, no. 3 (Fall 1975): 24–26.
Thinks Petry's short story addresses the illusions of assimilation and the prejudices that may exist among middle-class African-Americans. Calls the short story social protest, but with a "balanced perspective."

251 Maja-Pearce, Adewale. "Beyond Blackness." *Times Literary Supplement* (London), 2 May 1986, 479.
Considers Zora Neale Hurston and Petry to be "significant American writers of the [twentieth] century," primarily because they are truthful to

their visions and because they move beyond the rhetoric of race in, respectively, *Their Eyes Were Watching God* and *The Street.*

252   Mann, L. S. "Ann Petry's Novel of Negro and White in New England Community." *Springfield Republican,* 13 September 1953, 8.

Writes that there are "two powerful stories" in conflict in *The Narrows*: the character study of Abbie Crunch and a tragic love affair between Link Williams and Camilo Sheffield—a black man and a white woman. Finds fault with Petry's characterization of Link as a tragic figure. Says, instead, a character like Abbie "awakens this emotion."

253   Martin, Allie Beth. Review of *Tituba of Salem Village. Library Journal* 89 (15 September 1964): 3498.

Summarizes the plot very briefly. Thinks work will entice young people to read other works with similar themes.

254   Maund, Alfred. "The Negro Novelist and the Contemporary Scene." *Chicago Jewish Forum* 13 (Fall 1954): 28–34.

Assesses Petry's achievements in *The Street* and *The Narrows.* Considers *The Street* to be slightly "feminist." Thinks of Lutie as "the female counterpart" to Bigger Thomas. Likes the differing ways in which Petry handles the theme of "the idle rich" in both novels.

255   Meldon, John. "'The Street'—A Powerful Novel of Harlem Tragedy." *Daily Worker* (New York), 20 March 1946, 11.

Urges audiences to read *The Street* without delay. Says the novel shows white Americans how others might see them. Calls the novel a "shock treatment" for complacent white Americans. Applauds Petry for telling "the truth"—that is, for telling what is good and what is bad about her race. Dislikes, however, the novel's "too pessimistic" ending.

256   Moody, J. N. Review of *The Street. Commonweal,* 43 (22 February 1946): 486.

Questions whether a white girl as attractive as the protagonist might not have encountered tragic circumstances similar to those experienced by black protagonist Lutie. Argues against blaming Lutie's handicaps on race hatred. Applauds Petry, however, for her "sensitivity to detail" and for her ability to tell a powerful story.

257   Moon, Bucklin. "Both Sides of the Street." *New Republic* 114 (11 February 1946): 193–194.

Thinks Petry's "feeling of inner warmth and understanding" makes her characters come alive. Calls her bar scenes, however, contrived. Introduces the notion that Petry could become a pulp writer.

258 Morris, M. Aldon. Review of *Country Place. Boston Chronicle,* 22 May
1948 [Petry Collection, Schomburg].
Calls the theme "commonplace and the characters not too articulate."
Says, however, Petry holds the reader's attention "down to the very last
word of the book."

259 Morris, Wright. "The Complexity of Evil." *New York Times Book Review,*
Section 7, 16 August 1953, 4.
Calls parts of *The Narrows* disappointing and more of a "first draft."
Thinks, however, that parts of the novel are imaginative and credible. Sug-
gests a comparison between Mamie Powther and James Joyce's Molly
Bloom.

260 Morrison, Allan. "Women in the Arts." *Ebony* (August 1966): 90–94.
Provides a who's who of African-American women in literature, music, dance, and sculpture. Recognizes Petry among a small group of novelists.

261 Morsberger, Robert E. "The Further Transformation of Tituba." *New England Quarterly* 48, no. 3 (September 1974): 456–458.
Discusses Petry as a historical revisionist. Considers Tituba in *Tituba
of Salem Village* to be a "new addition to the pantheon of black heroines."

262 Nance, Merle. "Four-Star Novel." *People's Voice,* 16 February 1946, S–6.
Calls *The Street* a "novel of circumstances." Compares Petry's work
with Hardy's *Return of the Native,* saying that like Egdon Heath, the street
"is the acting." Believes Petry "builds her plot [and] interweaves her characters with an architectural solidity." Defends Petry against those critics
who claim she is defeatist. Writes that she merely fails to render solutions at
the end of her novel.

263 Nichols, Charles H. "New England Narrative." *Phylon* 14, no. 4 (Fourth
Quarter 1953): 437.
Criticizes Petry's style, calling its overall effect somewhat "disappointing," particularly with its lack of "profound emotional involvement."
Because of the novel's questioning of integrity and personal conviction,
moral values, and materialistic standards, however, considers it more than a
novel about race.

264 ———. "The Forties: A Decade of Growth." *Phylon* 11, no. 4 (Fourth
Quarter 1950): 377–380.
Says Petry's literary achievements as well as the literary achievements
of other African-American writers are attributable to the knowledge of craft
and "varieties of subject matters."

265 Noble, Jeanne. *Beautiful, Also, Are the Souls of My Black Sisters: A History of the Black Woman in America.* Englewood Cliffs, NJ: Prentice-Hall, 1978.

Traces literary developments of African-American women from domestic workers to self-sustaining individuals. When discussing the African-American woman as the domestic worker, Petry's Pink from "In Darkness and Confusion" and Lutie from early portions of *The Street* are included. Noble regards *The Street* as an early work that "Speak[s] the Truth to the People" about African-American women and their "struggles in the urban setting."

266 O'Banner, Bessie Marie. "A Study of Black Heroines in Four Selected Novels (1929–1959) by Four Black American Women Novelists: Zora Neale Hurston, Nella Larsen, Paule Marshall, Ann Lane Petry." *DAI* 43 (1981): 447A. Southern Illinois University at Carbondale.

Investigates the "old preoccupation' of blacks trying to "make it" according to white standards. Concludes that such standards found in Nella Larsen's *Passing* are replaced by concerns for "self-fulfillment," particularly with black women in Zora Neale Hurston's *Their Eyes Were Watching God,* Ann Petry's *The Street,* and Paule Marshall's *Brown Girl, Brownstones.*

267 O'Conner, Patricia T. Review of *The Street. New York Times Book Review,* 5 January 1986, 26.

Announces the reprint of *The Street.* Reiterates the novel's favorable reception in 1946 with quotes from numerous reviews that followed the 1946 publication. Reemphasizes Petry's strong characterizations.

268 Olsen, Tillie. "One Out of Twelve: Writers Who Are Women in Our Century." In *Silences.* New York: Delacorte/Seymour Lawrence, 1965. Reprint. 1972. Reprint. 1978.

Questions the domestic and literary lives of women writers in the twentieth century, and why only one out of twelve achieves critical recognition equal to that of men. Contends that many women are "silenced" by the "traditional silencers of humanity: class, color, gender," or by other silencers: "imposed guilt," or the fact that "a man can give full energy to his profession, a woman cannot." Discusses women as writers who "work on a paid job," "who are mothers as well as writers," or whose "books of great worth suffer the death of being unknown or, at best a peculiar eclipsing." Petry is one of the women mentioned.

269 "On the Author." *New York Herald Tribune Book Review,* Section 6, 16 August 1953, 2.

Offers quotes by the author about her experiences as a newspaperwoman and as a recreation field specialist in New York, how she came to win a Houghton Mifflin Fellowship Award, and what writers continue to influence her.

270   Ottley, Roi. "Famous People." Review of *Harriet Tubman, Conductor on the Underground Railroad. Chicago Sunday Tribune,* 13 November 1955, Part 4, Section 2, 50.

  Offers quotes by Petry on why she wrote Harriet Tubman's biography. Calls the biography "superb . . . [and] starkly honest."

271   "Out of a Fog." *Newsweek* (17 August 1953): 94–95.

  Calls Petry's setting in *The Narrows* theatrical and her style "subdued lyricism." Considers Petry's subsidiary characters, with their "long memories and frozen poetry," to be the most interesting.

272   Page, Ernest R. "Black Literature and Changing Attitudes: Does It Do the Job?" *English Journal* 66, no. 3 (March 1977): 29–33.

  As part of his Ph.D. dissertation, Page reveals the success of high school teachers who use African-American literature to "change . . . negative attitudes towards blacks." Includes in his "A Black Literature Package (BLP)," one novel, seven short stories, eight poems, one play, and five portions of autobiographies. Petry's short story "In Darkness and Confusion" is included.

273   Page, James A. "Black Literature." *English Journal* 62, no. 5 (May 1973): 709–717.

  Writes that "[some] of the best novel-writing of the 1940s [is] done by two women." Cites Petry as one of the two for *Country Place.*

274   ———. *Selected Black American Authors: An Illustrated Bio-Bibliography.* Boston: G. K. Hall, 1977.

  Petry is included.

275   Pappy, Esther Walls. Review of *Harriet Tubman, Conductor on the Underground Railroad. Saturday Review of Literature* (12 November 1955): 75.

  Contends that the style in *Harriet Tubman* is "quiet and evocative." Briefly compares the work with other biographies on Tubman, calling all others "meager." Calls Petry's summation of related historical events at the end of each chapter an attractive feature.

276   Parson, Margaret. "Absorbing Story of Negro Section in N. E. Town." *Telegram,* 16 August 1953 [Special Collections, Boston University].

  Reviews *The Narrows.* Finds Petry's "vivid and sensitive" portrayals of various characters more absorbing than the main plot. Along with a brief plot summary, concludes that the book is "strong in its ideas."

277 Peden, William H. "Of War and Peace and Other Matters." In *The American Short Story: Front Line in the National Defense of Literature.* Boston: Houghton Mifflin, 1964.

Identifies Petry's "Miss Muriel" along with short stories by James Baldwin, Frank Yerby, and Paule Marshall as "really good recent stories by and about American Negroes."

278 Peden, William. "The Black Explosion." *Studies in Short Fiction* 12, no. 3 (Summer 1975): 231–241.

Surveys and then recommends collections of modern short stories by African-American writers—from Langston Hughes to Henry Dumas. Recommends with explanations Petry's *Miss Muriel and Other Stories,* particularly "Miss Muriel," "The New Mirror," and "Mother Africa."

279 "Pile Them under the Tree." *Christian Century* (16 December 1970): 1516.

Gives a one-sentence review of *Legends of the Saints*: calls it "refreshing."

280 Poirier, Suzanne. "From Pharmacist to Novelist." In *Pharmacy in History,* 27–33. Madison, WI: American Institute of the History of Pharmacy, 1986.

Discusses the role of the pharmacist in several of Petry's short stories and in *Country Place.* Traces the development of one recurring theme that is relevant to Petry as well as to her characters who are pharmacists—distinctions between professional and private lives.

281 Pollock, Channing. "The Problem of Poverty" *Pictorial Review* (2 June 1946): 2:P.

Prompted by a scene from *The Street* in which Petry indicts society for the death of a jobless and starving black man, Pollock, citing facts and statistics, argues that poverty "is as old as civilization" and has yet to be solved with a redistribution of wealth.

282 Poore, Charles. "Books of the Times." *New York Times Book Review,* 7 February 1946, 21.

Suggests that because of Petry's convincing scenes and characters, her readers, regardless of race, "won't forget that Harlem street." Is convinced that the goodness of Lutie and Bub gives this mother and son superiority over the other characters.

283 Poston, Ted. "Cheers for Ann Petry—Good Job!" *New York Post,* 23 August 1953 [Petry Collection, Schomburg].

Looks briefly at Petry's characters in *The Narrows.* Says above all, Petry's characters, who just happen to be black, have problems and concerns that are common to all people.

284 Prescott, Orville. "Outstanding Novels." *Yale Review* 35 (Spring 1946): 574–575.

Writes that the problems of African-Americans in Harlem "are illuminated through the characters and not the other way round." Calls the characters "significantly individualistic" with their own "savagely engrossing" stories. Believes Petry's success lies in part in her "brutal frankness."

285 Price, Emerson. "Tragedy in Harlem." *Cleveland Press,* 12 February 1946 [Special Collections, Boston University].

Compares *The Street* with Richard Wright's *Native Son* and Chester Himes's *If He Hollers Let Him Go.* Says Petry's novel is "artistically superior." Also says Petry, unlike "most women writers . . . skillfully interprets the profoundest of human emotions."

286 "Prospects: LeRoi Jones?" In *Native Sons.* Edited by Edward Margolies. Philadelphia: Lippincott, 1968.

Mentions Petry favorably. Notes the importance of a writer such as Petry including in her works "technical proficiency and a freshness of outlook."

287 Pryse, Marjorie. "'Patterns against the Sky': Deism and Motherhood in Ann Petry's *The Street.*" In *Conjuring: Black Women, Fiction, and Literary Tradition.* Edited by Marjorie Pryse and Hortense J. Spillers. Bloomington: Indiana University Press, 1985.

Writes that Petry uses language in *The Street* that "evokes a deistic universe." Within this universe, there are "laws" of the street, set in motion by white people. Pryse contends, however, that there are other forces that counter these laws—Lutie's Granny, Mrs. Hedges, and Prophet David. Concludes that Petry's novel offers "its readers an alternative in the vision of a black community which might embrace its grandmothers, its folklore, and the survival of human feeling."

288 Purdy, Theodore M. "The Ghetto that is Harlem." *Saturday Review of Literature* (2 March 1946):30.

Thinks Petry "stacks the cards unfairly" against Lutie, particularly when Petry fails to show how "the street" changes and deforms the lives of the more seditious characters in the novel.

289 Puri, Usha. *Towards a New Womanhood: A Study of Black Women Writers.* Jaipur, India: Printwell, 1989.

Offers critical interpretations of Petry's fiction.

290 Rayson, Ann. Ann Petry. In *American Women Writers: A Critical Reference Guide from Colonial Times to the Present.* Edited by Langdon Lynne Faust. Vol. 2, M to Z. New York: Frederick Ungar, 1983. First printed in 1979.

Agrees with those critics who say *The Street* is "gripping yet simplistic," with those who say *Country Place* is Petry's "most successful novel," and with those who say *The Narrows* is "simultaneously sophisticated and melodramatic." Believes Petry's short stories succeed better than her novels. Calls for more thorough criticism of all her works.

291 Redding, J. Saunders. Review of *The Narrows. Afro-American* (Baltimore), 12 September 1953, 2.

Compares *The Narrows* to Petry's first and second novels and concludes that it shows "greater narrative skill" than the first and "tighter, sounder thematic structure" than the second. Says Petry's works suggest she has been working toward a "creative philosophy" and an "artistic creed." Calls one element of Petry's creed and philosophy "realistic idealism"—that is, she writes as if there are no fundamental differences between the races.

292 ———. "The Problem of the Negro Writer." *Massachusetts Review* (Autumn–Winter 1964): 57–70. Reprint. *Black and White in American Culture: An Anthology from the Massachusetts Review.* Edited by Jules Chametzky and Sidney Kaplan. Amherst: University of Massachusetts Press, 1969.

Concludes that the problem of dual commitment created by African-American writers for themselves can be transcended "positively." For example, Saunders looks to Petry and Ralph Ellison "with a recognition of the fact that Negro behavior—character, sensation, thought—is dredged from the same deep mine of potentials that is the source of all human behavior."

293 Reid, Margaret Walraven. Review of *Harriet Tubman, Conductor on the Underground Railroad. Library Journal* 80 (15 September 1955): 45.

Recommends the work highly. Calls it historical, objective, and superior, especially when compared with previous books on Harriet Tubman.

294 "Remember Salem?" *Old Saybrook Pictorial,* 28 January 1970, 30.

Repeats much that is said in other articles about what influenced Petry's writing of *Tituba.*

295 Review of *Country Place. New Yorker* (11 October 1947): 122.

Concludes that the novel's ending is plagued by a "couple of improbabilities." Also concludes that Petry has joined other novelists who write about the "bigotry, marital infidelity, and astounding malice" that exist in the American small town.

296 Review of *Country Place. Wisconsin Library Bulletin.* 43 (November 1947): 154.

Provides a very brief review of *Country Place.* Offers plot summary and concludes that the novel is "completely different ... from *The Street.*"

297 Review of *Harriet Tubman, Conductor on the Underground Railroad. Best Sellers* 30 (1 February 1971): 482–483.

Announces under subtitle "History and Biography" that *Harriet Tubman* has been released in paperback. Calls the biography a "great story."

298 Review of *Harriet Tubman, Conductor on the Underground Railroad. Booklist* 52 (15 September 1955): 39.

Calls the biography a "lifelike and poignant portrait."

299 Review of *Harriet Tubman, Conductor on the Underground Railroad. Commonweal* 63 (18 November 1955): 182.

Concludes in one sentence that the biography has been written skillfully and warmly.

300 Review of *Harriet Tubman, Conductor on the Underground Railroad. Grade Teacher* (September 1971): 158, 160.

Announces that the biography is now in paperback. Calls the work "good news in Black history." Says that Petry's book is more in-depth compared with other biographies on Tubman.

301 Review of *Harriet Tubman, Conductor on the Underground Railroad. New Yorker* (26 November 1955): 216. [Also appears in some issues with different page number—p. 228.]

In both issues, Tubman's biographer is said to provide an "evocative portrait."

302 Review of *Legends of the Saints. Horn Book Magazine* (December 1970): 611.

Criticizes author's writing style, calling it flat. Is impressed, however, with the expressive illustrations and the scholarly research in *Legends of the Saints.*

303 Review of *Legends of the Saints. Kirkus* 38 (15 October 1970): 1137.

Says the book expresses "human integrity" and the greatness of the "traditional hero."

304 Review of *Legends of the Saints. Library Journal* 96 (15 January 1971): 44.

Praises the book's form, calling it familiar, significant, and pleasing.

305 Review of *Miss Muriel and Other Stories. Booklist* 68 (15 September 1971): 83.

Finds the stories about the Layen family to be "fresh and poignant," but considers some of the other stories, especially those with ghetto settings, to be less than appealing.

306   Review of *Miss Muriel and Other Stories. Kirkus* 34, no. 11 (1 June 1971): 587.

Criticizes Petry's style in *Miss Muriel,* calling it "not quite up to rough-grained urban realities." Concludes, however, that overall the collection is "superb."

307   Review of *Miss Muriel and Other Stories. Library Journal* 96 (July 1971): 2348.

Encourages librarians to display the collection. Calls it evocative with descriptive writings.

308   Review of *Miss Muriel and Other Stories. Library Journal* (Special Section), 96 (November 1971): 3915.

Emphasizes that while Petry's stories in this collection first appear in magazines from the 1940s, they "still have appeal for today's readers." Contends Petry has a well-founded view of characters and their communities.

309   Review of *Miss Muriel and Other Stories. Publishers' Weekly* (12 July 1971): 66.

With the exception of her stories set in Harlem, which reviewer finds didactic, Petry is said to be in absolute control of her material. Describes her stories as being "exquisitely" composed.

310   Review of *The Drugstore Cat. Booklist* 46 (15 November 1949): 105.

Promises that the adventures in the book will entertain younger children.

311   Review of *The Drugstore Cat. New York Herald Tribune Book Review,* Section 7, November 1949, 13.

Concludes the book has a "fresh, sensitive and witty" style. Feels that the story about a cat who learns to "control" his temper provides a moral for its young readers.

312   Review of *The Drugstore Cat. Saturday Review of Literature* (12 November 1949): 32.

Provides a very brief summary of plot. Praises Petry's narrative and drawings by Susanne Suba.

313   Review of *The Narrows. American Literature* 60, no. 4 (December 1988): 709.

Announces the reprint of *The Narrows.* Calls the new Introduction by Nellie McKay "convincingly appreciative" and capable of rekindling "interest" in the work.

314 Review of the *Narrows. Booklist* 50 (1 September 1953): 14.
     Describes Link's murder as "shameful." Praises Petry for writing a clear story about "good, misguided, [and] genuinely vicious" characters who are without personal "condemnations."

315 Review of *The Narrows. Catholic World* 178 (December 1953): 235.
     Thinks the structure of *The Narrows* is "thesis-laden." Calls the climax "incredible."

316 Review of *The Narrows. New Statesman and Nation* (London), 14 August 1954 [Special Collections, Boston University].
     Dislikes adamantly the use of flashback in *The Narrows*. Thinks Petry does a disservice to herself—the "first-rate story-teller"—with the flashback technique. Disapproves of Petry's portrayal of Camilo—the "only dull and unconvincing character" in the novel.

317 Review of *The Narrows. New Yorker* (29 August 1953): 78.
     Criticizes Petry's style and structure, particularly her many points of view, her "impossibilities" in characters, and her melodramatic ending. Concludes, however, Malcolm Powther is a "beautifully constructed character."

318 Review of *The Narrows. Star* (Washington, DC), 16 August 1953 [Special Collections, Boston University].
     Calls Petry an "extremely gifted writer," who has the "eye and ear of the born novelist." But contends that in spite of her "vibrant narrative," her "observation and humor," and her "richness of character"—like Abbie Crunch the Treadway butler, the newspaper editor, and Camilo—*The Narrows* has its shortcomings. Those are interior monologues that are not in sync with the main dialogue and an improbable romance that allows its lovers to cross the color line.

319 Review of *The Narrows. Wisconsin Library Bulletin* 49 (September–October 1953): 212.
     Provides a very brief summary of plot.

320 Review of *The Street. Booklist* 42 (1 March 1946): 213–214.
     Provides a very brief plot summary. Comments on Petry's "remarkable lack of bitterness."

321 Review of *The Street. Catholic World* 163 (May 1946): 187.
     Calls *The Street* an extended short story. Predicts Petry's focus on sex and other vices will be objectionable to some African-American readers.

322 Review of *The Street. Columbus Citizen,* 24 February 1946 [Special Collections, Boston University].
Refers to Petry as an exemplar of "Negro realists" who demands from her race "higher codes of ethics"—as one of the "first steps" toward a better life. Same review appears in *Washington Post,* 17 February 1946.

323 Review of *The Street. Negro Story* 2 (April–May 1946): 65.
Calls *The Street* an "unforgettable indictment of a system that creates and perpetuates ghettos for its most wretched minority group, the Negro." Concludes the novel is "a must" for those who have escaped "the street' or who are unacquainted with it. Criticizes the novel for not having at least two "decent strong characters."

324 Review of *The Street. New Yorker* (9 February 1946): 98.
Declares the novel is "an oppressive but moving account" of Lutie Johnson's struggle to survive in Harlem and to retain her self-respect. Criticizes, however, Petry's "tendency to overwrite."

325 Review of *The Street. Washington Post,* 17 February 1946 [Special Collections, Boston University].
Refers to Petry as an exemplar of "Negro realists," who demands from her race "higher codes of ethics"—one of the "first steps" toward a better life.

326 Review of *The Street. Wisconsin Library Bulletin* 42 (April 1946): 60.
Provides a very brief plot summary. Calls the novel "well written . . . impressive and moving."

327 Review of *Tituba of Salem Village. Atlantic Monthly* (December 1964): 163.
Calls *Tituba* "an absorbing story."

328 Review of *Tituba of Salem Village. Booklist* 69 (1 May 1972): 839.
Considers the work a "good historical narrative based on fact."

329 Review of *Tituba of Salem Village. Saturday Review of Literature* (7 November 1964): 55.
Calls the book the strongest and the best written about witchcraft for young readers. Acknowledges Petry's research for the book. Summarizes the plot.

330 Rickman, Ray. "Ann Petry Revisited." *American Visions* 5 (February 1990): 56.
Anticipating new readership for Petry's reprinted novels and short stories, this writer revisits Petry through biography and select bibliography. Calls *The Street* a "forerunner" of works by Toni Morrison, Alice Walker, and Gloria Naylor.

331. Riis, Roger William. "A Story of 'Hemmed In' Lives." *Opportunity: Journal of Negro Life* 24, no. 3 (July–September 1946): 157.

Questions the "poetic distribution . . . poetic justice" in *The Street,* particularly when one unsuspecting character commits suicide on Christmas morning and when "half-way decent characters" end up "in jail or in flight" while wicked characters are left "flourishing."

332. Roberts, Margaret Olivia. "Writing to Liberate: Selected Black Women Novelists from 1859 to 1982," *DAI* 49 (1987): 506A. University of Maryland.

Contends that "in the nearly one hundred years between *Iola Leroy* and *The Color Purple,* the nature and kinds of oppression are described more graphically and the women suffer more intensely in the later works." When exploring reasons for this contradiction, particularly since history proves the 1890s were more restrictive and oppressive years for black women than the present, Roberts examines seven African-American novelists who wrote between *Iola Leroy* and *The Color Purple*. Petry (*The Street*) is included.

333. Robinson, Ted. "Reviews of the Latest Books, with Sidelights on Authors." *Cleveland Plain Dealer,* 24 February 1946, 14.

Warns the reader that there is "no palliating beauty . . . no optimistic philosophy, no relieving humor" in *The Street*. Says rather that there are conditions that "constitute national scandal."

334. Rogers, W. G. "Ann Petry's New Novel Disappointing." *New York Post,* 27 September 1947 [Special Collections, Boston University].

Disapproves of *Country Place*'s "unconvincing characters" and its lack of "great passion" as found in *The Street*.

335. Rosenblatt, Roger. "White Outside." In *Black Fiction*. Cambridge: Harvard University Press, 1974.

Contends that unlike most white writers, black writers have taken care "not to reduce [their] white characters to stereotypes." Rather, "there . . . emerges within black fiction a consistent picture of white America." Petry's characters in *Country Place* serve as examples.

336. Ross, Mary. "Depth and Dignity, Pathos and Humor." *New York Herald Tribune Book Review,* 16 August 1953, 3.

Summarizes the plot in *The Narrows*. Calls the work powerfully imaginative and deeply insightful. Insists the book is neither an "apologia for the Negro nor . . . an indictment of the white race."

337. Royster, Beatrice Horn. "The Ironic Vision of Four Black Women Novelists: A Study of the Novels of Jessie Fauset, Nella Larsen, Zora Neale Hurston, and Ann Petry." *DAI* 36 (1975): 8051A.

Says Jessie Fauset, Nella Larsen, Zora Neale Hurston, and Ann Petry write from "a black perspective, a female perspective, and a world perspective." Reacting differently to their worlds, the writers are said to display a range of unmistakable qualities of irony.

338 Ruffin, Carolyn F. "In All Shades of Black." *Christian Science Monitor,* 19 August 1971, 10.
Praises Petry for her objectivity, diversity, and lack of didacticism in her short stories found in *Miss Muriel and Other Stories.*

339 Schraufnagel, Noel. "The Protest Tradition in the Forties." In *The Black American Novel.* Deland, FL: Everett/Edwards, 1972.
Criticizes Petry's ending in *The Street,* citing psychological nuances that would have dictated an alternate ending. Thinks that with Lutie—a metaphysical rebel who is fallible—Petry destroys the black matriarch myth. Compares Petry's novel to other works that illustrate the "effects of environment and oppression on an individual." Summarizes the plot.
Calls *Country Place* an assimilationist novel, which, like *The Street,* places its characters against the hostile environment. Summarizes the plot.
Sees *The Narrows* as a combination of Petry's earlier attempts in her first two novels—that is, she reflects the effects of racism and analyzes the human condition. Summarizes the plot.

340 Seets, Myrthe Nancee. "The Maturation of the Negro Novelist as Revealed in the Novels of Richard Wright, Ann Petry, Chester Himes, and Frank Yerby." Master's thesis, Fisk University, 1949.
Analyzes and evaluates *The Street* and *Country Place,* particularly characters and plots.

341 Shinn, Thelma J. "Women in the Novels of Ann Petry." *Critique, Studies in Modern Fiction* 16, no. 1 (1974): 110–120.
Argues that in *The Street, Country Place* and *The Narrows,* "Petry shows . . . the sordidness of reality, the inequities and false illusions of society, and the inadequacies of the possibilities for women [black and white] . . . for personal development. . . ."

342 Shockley, Ann. *Living Black American Authors: A Biographical Directory.* New York: Bowker, 1973.
Includes Petry.

343 Showalter, Elaine. "Women and the Literary Curriculum." *College English* 32, no. 8 (May 1971): 855–866.
Illustrates how college women are estranged from their own experience because of the male-oriented reading lists being generated in general college literature classes. Provides as an alternative a "Syllabus for English 235: The Woman Writer in the 20th Century." Includes on the reading list, under black women writers, *The Street* by Ann Petry.

344 Sillen, Samuel. "Ann Petry's 'Country Place'—Novel of Small-Town Life." *Daily Worker,* 8 October 1947, 11.

Focuses primarily on summary of plot, characterization, and point of view, calling the former melodramatic and the latter confusing. Considers all the characters static, with the exception of Johnnie Roane.

345 Skeeter, Sharyn J. "Black Women Writers: Levels of Identity." *Essence* (May 1973): 58–59, 76, 89.

Chronologizes a literary tradition and "what Black women have written about themselves." Includes Petry's three novels. Also singles out *The Street* for its themes of marriage and motherhood, *Country Place* for its interpersonal relationships, and *The Narrows* for its ambition.

346 Smith, Barbara. "A Familiar Street." *Belles Lettres* (January/February 1987): 4.

Acknowledges the reprint of *The Street* with praise for what she calls a "classic if only because of its vivid descriptions, strong characterizations, and involving plot." Concludes that Petry inspires her readers to question the system that hinders Lutie from succeeding. As a reviewer/reader, Smith ends with similiar hope found in the novel—hope for political changes.

347 ———. "Doing Research on Black American Women." *Women's Studies Newsletter* 4 (Spring 1976): 4–7.

Provides ideas for doing research on black women writers. In addition, suggests thematic approaches to reading fiction by black women writers. Includes Petry's *The Street* under the following thematic approaches: "Independent Black Women," "Black Women and Black Men," and "Black Women Working."

348 ———. "Toward a Black Feminist Criticism." *Conditions: Two* 1, no. 2 (October 1977): 25–42. Reprint. *All the Women Are White, All the Blacks Are Men, But Some of Us Are Brave.* Edited by Gloria T. Hull, Patricia Bell Scott, and Barbara Smith. New York: The Feminist Press, 1982.

Contends that there is a need for a black feminist criticism. Cites examples of how male critics have misunderstood or misrepresented Petry's *The Street* due to the lack of an established black feminist critical perspective.

349 Smith, Bradford. "Glandular Imbalance." *Saturday Review of Literature* (18 October 1947): 17, 21.

Review of *Country Place.* Finds much fault with the novel: Says the "good" characters are "shadowy"; says the "bad" characters, beyond their lust or greed, "lack motivation or background." Concludes that often both "good" and "bad" characters are "at the mercy of their glands" and "cannot develop or change"; thus, the characters provide no basis for sympathy or emotional engagement from the reader. Says Petry's overall design of the novel is contrived and melodramatic.

350   Smith, Eleanor Touhey. Review of *The Narrows. Library Journal* 78 (July 1953): 1232.
      Proclaims that Petry's thesis concludes that cultural equality alone cannot erase "race" prejudice in America. Calls her plot and characterizations "absorbing."

351   Smith, Harrison. "Writers Are Unhappy." *Saturday Review of Literature* (28 December 1946): 16.
      Reviews Martha Foley's *The Best American Short Stories,* but includes brief review of Petry's "Like a Winding Sheet"—a short story included in Foley's collection. Calls the story "most forceful and memorable" but "funereally titled."

352   Smith, John Caswell, Jr. Review of *Country Place. Atlantic Monthly* 180 (November 1947): 178, 182.
      Gives a plot summary of the novel, emphasizing how the hurricane in the story "whip[s]" up the story's "onset, climax, and departure." Contrary to most critics, this reviewer thinks Johnnie is "not filled out to real-life believable proportions." In congruence with other critics, however, this reviewer finds the narration by the druggist to be a distracting technique.

353   ———. Review of *The Street. Atlantic Monthly* 117 (April 1946): 172.
      Reiterates Petry's accounts of the "instability of the Negro family" in the urban North. Says Petry's characters are only partially fictional, particularly when studies by sociologists can confirm that the black father cannot get adequate work and that black mothers, trying to keep the family intact, enter into the most available work outside of the home—domestic.

354   Southgate, Robert L. *Black Plots and Black Characters: A Handbook for Afro-American Literature.* Syracuse, NY: Gaylord Professional Publications, 1979.
      Provides a summational analysis, particularly of plot in *The Street.* Is briefly bibliographical.

355   Springer, Gertrude. Review of *The Street. Survey Graphic* 35, no. 6 (June 1946): 230–231.
      Criticizes the novel for suggesting that its setting is the epitome of "all of Harlem." Says Lutie is "not very smart," primarily because she fails to turn her hatred into productive ways to use the white people and their institutions for her own purposes.

356 Stannard, Dorothy. Review of *The Street. Punch* (London), (12 February 1986): 72.

Announces the reprint of *The Street.* Calls the novel "grim realism." Thinks the plot helps to place the work within the "Hardyesque chain of doom." Also says Lutie has the "depth and poignancy of a Tess."

357 Starke, Catherine Juanita. *Black Portraiture in American Fiction: Stock Characters, Archetypes, and Individuals.* New York: Basic Books, 1971.

Considers Lutie to be an archetype, calling her a "sacrifi[cial] symbol or victim of cultural and environmental determinism."

358 Stepto, Robert B. "I Thought I Knew These People: Richard Wright and the Afro-American Literary Tradition." In *Chant of Saints: A Gathering of Afro-American Literature, Art, and Scholarship.* Edited by Michael S. Harper and Robert B. Stepto. Chicago: University of Illinois Press, 1979.

Examines Richard Wright's place or "lack of one" in the African-American literary tradition. Points to African-American women writers whose works revise the Mrs. Thomases, Bessies, and Bigger Thomases. For example, Petry is thought to have been "about the task not only of redeeming Bessie but of revising Bigger as well."

359 Stewart, Carolyn H. *Midwest Journal* 6, no. 1 (Spring 1954): 4–5.

Takes a formalistic approach to *The Narrows.* Writes that "the form of the narrative reinforces the sense of leisurely, spontaneous development." Concludes, however, that due to structural interruptions, the love story between Link and Camilo is "deprived of emotional continuity and intensity." Nonetheless, finds Petry to be honest and fresh in her approach to inter- and intraracial conflicts.

360 Streitfeld, David. "Petry's Brew: Laughter and Fury." *Washington Post,* 25 February 1992, E1–E2.

Interweaves biography, bibliography, and comments by Petry and her daughter into a lengthy and intriguing introduction (or reintroduction) to the writer and her first novel, *The Street*—first published in 1946 by Houghton Mifflin and now being reissued. Two recent photographs are included.

361 Sullivan, Oona. Review of *Legends of the Saints. New York Times Book Review,* 29 November 1970.

With the exception of the story of Saint Christopher, calls Petry's stories about saints "a bit tall."

362 Sullivan, Richard. "Injustice, Out of Focus." *New York Times Book Review,* 28 September 1947, 12.

Compares *Country Place* to *The Street,* calling the former "quiet . . . carefully and economically phrased." Dismisses the "switched point of view" as a weakness. Hails the novel's style, calling it "bright and vigorous." Hails the novel's characterizations, calling them "forceful."

363   Svendsen, Kester. "Another Negro Family Finding Life Too Harsh." *Daily Oklahoman,* 24 February 1946 [Special Collections, Boston University].

Calls *The Street* not just another problem novel. Says "any honest novel about the Negro is almost inevitably a racial problem novel." Notes how Petry avoids the "stereotyped" and the "symbolic" problem novel. Emphasizes that Lutie searches for "a home and security" but fails to secure either, in part because she lives in the ghetto.

364   Taylor, Ivan E. Review of *The Narrows. Current Literature* 23 no. 1 (Winter 1954): 60–61.

Discusses many critical aspects of *The Narrows*: its explosive themes; its humor; its commonplaceness yet universality; and its use of propaganda, particularly its commentary on how daily newspapers manipulate news about crimes committed by African-Americans.

365   Trilling, Diana. "Class and Color." *The Nation* 162 (9 March 1946): 290–291.

Reviews Petry's *The Street* and Fannie Cook's *Mrs. Palmer's Honey.* Concludes that neither "challenges the prestige of Lillian Smith's *Strange Fruit.*" Thinks, however, *The Street* states better than *Mrs. Palmer's Honey* that "class feelings are as firmly ingrained in the colored population . . . as in the white."

366   "'The Street' Still Unchanged." *Hartford Courant,* 7 March 1969, 32.

Offers quotes by Petry who concludes that after thirty years, she could write the same book about "any American ghetto." The writer reaffirms her reasons for writing *The Street.*

367   Troupe, Quincy. "A Conversation with Terry McMillan." *Emerge* (October 1992): 51–56.

When asked to name her literary influences, McMillan includes Petry. Says Petry, in *The Street,* taught her to write in her own voice.

368   Turner, Darwin T. "'The Negro Novel in America'; In Rebuttal." *CLA Journal* 10, no. 2 (December 1966): 122–134.

Refutes a number of Robert Bone's inferences, including his statement that writers like Petry who wrote the non-Negro novel were "Assimilationists[s]."

369   V. P. H. "New England Novel Fine Despite Central Theme Flaw." *World Herald* (Omaha), 6 September 1953 [Special Collections, Boston University].

Suggests Petry entwines the past—Abbie who symbolizes "all the old-fashioned virtues"—with the present, a romance. Finds faults with Petry's present. Thinks that the interracial love affair between Link and Camilo is almost totally "unconvincing" because of the times. Insists *The Narrows* is not a "race novel" but a "New England novel" of spirit.

370 Van Dore, Edrie. "Yankees Bear South's Social Problem." *Hartford Times,* 15 August 1953 [Special Collections, Boston University].

Acknowledges Link and Camilo for their courage, but thinks Camilo was never in love with Link. Encourages critical attention to the minor aspects of the novel, particularly the "casual romancing" of Mamie Powther and the "prim uprightness of the typical New England widow Abbie Crunch." Insists the unexpected and violent ending of the novel has deeper meaning, particularly in terms of black-white relationships in the North.

371 Varga-Coley, Barbara Jean. "The Novels of Black American Women." *DAI* 42 (1981): 707A. State University of New York at Stony Brook.

Looks at what might be considered similar African-American experiences that have been examined in novels by a host of African-American women writers.

372 Vechten, Carl Van. "A Portfolio of Photographs." In *Amistad 2.* Edited by John A. Williams and Charles F. Harris. New York: Random House, 1971.

Includes a photograph of Petry from the 1940s.

373 "Violence against Black Women." In *All the Women Are White, All the Blacks Are Men, But Some of Us Are Brave.* Edited by Gloria T. Hull, Patricia Bell Scott, and Barbara Smith. Old Westbury, NY: The Feminist Press, 1982.

Holds that violence is largely against the woman because of her "position under patriarchy," and that "black men as well as white men violate and attack her." Uses as an example, under the subcategory "Battering," Petry's female victim from "Like a Winding Sheet."

374 Voiles, Jane. "A Bookman's Notebook." *San Francisco Chronicle,* 19 December 1947 [Special Collections, Boston University].

Provides a very brief review of *Country Place.* Basically disapoves of the novel's melodrama and its lack of "stark dramatic quality."

375 ———. "Bookman's Notebook." *San Francisco Chronicle,* 26 August 1953, 17.

Criticizes the style of *The Narrows,* particularly its "overworked flashback soliloquies ... and [its] long redundant passages." Concludes, however, that Petry "knows her race, its strength and its weakness."

376   Wade-Gayles, Gloria. "Going Nowhere Immediate." In *No Crystal Stair: Visions of Race and Sex in Black Women's Fiction.* New York: The Pilgrim Press, 1984.

Focuses on black women characters who are "overworked in menial jobs, underpaid, humiliated, used, abused, and ignored." From *The Street,* she looks to Min and Mrs. Hedges as examples.

377   ———. "Journeying from Can't to Can and Sometimes Back to 'Can't.'" In *No Crystal Stair: Visions of Race and Sex in Black Women's Fiction.* New York: The Pilgrim Press, 1984.

Defends with in-depth analysis the thesis that *The Street* is not a "carbon copy" of *Native Son.* Calls Petry's novel "an explosion of the sounds of racial and sexual agony."

378   ———. "She Who Is Black and Mother: In Sociology and Fiction, 1940–1970." In *The Black Woman.* Edited by La Frances Rodgers-Rose. Beverly Hills, CA: Sage, 1980.

Suggests correlating Petry's *The Street* with sociological studies by sociologist Frazier. Says the divergent paths of the sociologist and novelist "intersect and converge" and that specifics from "real life" can "add weight" to and "enlarge the imaginative realities" in Petry's novel.

379   ———. "The Narrow Space and the Dark Enclosure: Race and Sex in the Lives of Black Women in Selected Novels Written by Black Women, 1946–1976." *DAI* 42 (1981): 2736A. Emory University.

Examines the African-American woman within an enduring racist and capitalistic society, or within a "narrow space" as mother, as woman of hopelessness, and as woman who struggles for wider options in her life.

380   Warfel, Harry R. Ann Petry. In *American Novelists of Today.* New York: American Book Company, 1951.

Biographical and bibliographical. Several dates, however, are incorrect.

381   Washington, Gladys J. "A World Made Cunningly: A Closer Look at Ann Petry's Short Fiction." *CLA Journal* 30, no. 1 (September 1986): 14–29.

Takes a comprehensive look at style, structure, and characterization in Petry's short stories found in *Miss Muriel and Other Stories.* Concludes that the stories might be divided into two distinctive groups: those that depict a "small-town world with people enjoying simple pleasures" and those that depict the inner city and "all the tensions and frustrations ... associated with the urban scene." Thinks Petry's characters reflect "a multiplicity of tendencies, attitudes, desires, and determinations." Calls Petry's world one that is crafted with the skill of artistry by a writer "keenly attuned to the nuances of [the] world about her."

382 Washington, Mary Helen. "Black Women Image Makers." *Black World* 23, no. 10 (August 1974): 11.

Believes African-American women writers are projecting "powerful" and "realistic" images that combat stereotypes of black women. Names Petry as one of those writers.

383 ———. "'Infidelity Becomes Her': The Ambivalent Woman in the Fiction of Ann Petry." In *Invented Lives: Narratives of Black Women, 1860–1960.* Garden City, NY: Anchor/Doubleday, 1987.

Criticizes Petry's "insistence on environmental determinism as an explanation for her characters' dead-end lives." Says such an approach ignores "deeply felt realities" such as women's "relationships with their families," women's "own suppressed creativity," or women's "conflicts with black men and with patriarchy." Concludes that in *The Street* and in "In Darkness and Confusion," Petry writes about Harlem "as an outsider," but in a story like "Miss Muriel," Petry is "the insider [with] a vantage point of power which her characters share."

384 ———. "Teaching *Black-Eyed Susans: An Approach to the Study of Black Women Writers.*" *CLA Journal* 11, no. 1 (Spring 1977): 23. *All the Women Are White, All the Blacks Are Men, But Some of Us Are Brave.* Reprint. Edited by Gloria T. Hull, Patricia Bell Scott, and Barbara Smith. Old Westbury, NY: The Feminist Press, 1982.

Provides suggestions for thematic approaches to the study of literature by African-American women writers. Suggests Lutie from *The Street* be placed under the subcategory "The Suspended Woman."

385 Watkins, Mel. "Sexism, Racism and Black Women Writers." *New York Times Book Review,* 15 June 1986, 1, 35–37.

Argues that since the 1960s, the feminist movement, and the publication of *The Flagellants,* black women writers have had much impact on American literature. Yet, in spite of their "ascendancy and success," they have persisted in their negative portrayals of black men. Notes that talented black women writers such as Ann Petry, Alice Childress, and Paule Marshall "who . . . have avoided these attacks [these negative portrayals] have not been as successful." See Number 149 for a rebuttal.

386 Watson, Carole McAlpine. *Prologue: The Novels of Black American Women, 1891–1965.* Westport, CT: Greenwood, 1985.

Provides analyses and annotated bibliographies for fifty-eight of the sixty-four novels written between 1891 and 1965 by African-American women. Chapter III, which deals with "works of universal meaning," includes a discussion of Petry's *The Narrows.*

387 Weir, Sybil. "'The Narrows': A Black New England Novel." *Studies in American Fiction* 15, no. 1 (Spring 1987): 81–93.

Claims that Petry's *The Narrows* illustrates the writer's indebtedness to Nathaniel Hawthorne and Richard Wright, to New England women writers, and to her experiences in Harlem in the 1940s. Says *The Narrows* provokes African-American realities, particularly the blues tradition, double consciousness, or African-Americans with "two souls" (one American, the other African), and the support of the community.

388 Whitbeck, Doris. "Women Artists at U Conn Fest." *Hartford Courant,* 25 March 1979, IG, 5G.

Announces guest artists for a week-long arts festival at the University of Connecticut. Highlights Petry's participation and provides tidbits about her family, career, and specific writings.

389 Whitlow, Roger. "1940–1960: Urban Realism and Beyond." In *Black American Literature: A Critical History.* Chicago: Nelson-Hall, 1973. Revised. 1976.

Convinced that *The Street,* like *Native Son,* is concerned with the "effects of environment . . . on people," this writer compares Lutie to Bigger Thomas. Calls Lutie "trapped" and reactionary. Places Petry in the "urban realism" movement.

390 Williams, Sherley Anne. Review of *the Street. MS* 23 (September 1986): 23.

Announces the reprint of *The Street.* Says the "real power" of the novel lies in Petry's ability to understand the "roles that gender and sexuality play in the exploitation of black women." Claims the novel earns Petry "an abiding place among American naturalist novelists."

391 Wilson, Mark. "A MELUS Interview: Ann Petry—The New England Connection." *MELUS* 15, no. 2 (Summer 1988): 71–84.

Discusses Petry's role as storyteller in both her short and long fiction. (See full interview in this bibliography.)

392 "Witchcraft Topic for Author's Talk." *Middletown Press,* 17 January 1970 [Special Collections, Boston University].

Duplicates information in other articles explaining how Petry came to write *Tituba.*

393 Wolfe, Barbara. "'The Narrows' Breeds Life Full of Turmoil, Confusion." *Star* (Indianapolis), 13 September 1953 [Special Collections, Boston University].

Thinks Petry should have ended her story halfway through the novel. As it is, the novel becomes anticlimactic and melodramatic. Wolfe calls Abbie and Link detailed characterizations, but says Powther and his wife Mamie warrant "exclusive attention."

394 Wormley, Margaret Just. Review of *Country Place. Current Literature* 17, no. 2 (Spring 1948): 169.

Contends that "in an age in which we aim to support the thesis of one world, it is wholesome to note that some Negro creative artists [e.g., Petry] are apparently concerned with Art." Concludes that *Country Place,* with its "compactness of style, increased fluidity of dialogue, and convincing character analysis," is a "marked advance" over *The Street.*

395 "Writer Credits Success to Customers of Father's Old Saybrook Drugstore." *Hartford Courant,* 26 September 1947, 1.

Offered are quotes by Petry to suggest that the druggist-narrator in *Country Place* is her "father made over," that the novel's setting is "partly that of Old Saybrook," and that the characters in the novel are like the customers who came into her father's drugstore.

396 Yarborough, Richard. "The Quest for the American Dream in Three Afro-American Novels: *If He Hollers Let Him Go, The Street,* and *Invisible Man. MELUS* 8, no. 4 (Winter 1981): 33–59.

Writes that after "four decades of innumerable promises upon which America has almost inevitably reneged, the dialectical tension in Afro-American thought between hope and despair begins to produce a new synthesis: the agonizing recognition that white racism may forever keep the American Dream out of the black's grasp." To support this thesis, Yarborough points to reactions evoked by the failure of the Dream in Petry's *The Street,* Himes's *If He Hollers,* and Ellison's *Invisible Man.*

397 Yates, Elizabeth. "To Freedom by the Underground." *Christian Science Monitor,* 25 August 1955, 11.

Provides a brief review of *Harriet Tubman.*

398 Yglesias, Jose. "A Classy-Type People." *New Masses,* 9 December 1947 [Special Collections, Boston University].

Provides a lengthy critique of *Country Place,* focusing on Petry's "matter-of-fact" style and her "familiar" characters. Questions whether *Country Place* is a "morality tale."

Interviews

Ann Petry Talks about First Novel
James W. Ivey

One day in October, 1943, I was going through a batch of manuscripts when I picked out one with the teasing title "On Saturday the Siren Sounds at Noon." It turned out upon examination to be a short story by Ann Petry. I had not known the name before, but a glance at the first paragraph told me that the woman was a writer. I went to my editor with enthusiastic praise for the story and we both agreed that it was "good stuff" and should be printed. We scheduled the story for our December, 1943, issue. This was the first published story of a young writer of remarkable talent. Further interest was aroused in the story when one of the editors of the publishing house of Houghton Mifflin asked for copies of the December issue.

This was my first introduction to the writings of Mrs. Petry. But I never met Mrs. Petry until the winter of 1946, almost three years later. In the meantime, she had submitted for publication a long-short story on the Harlem riot of August, 1943. Though a brilliant psychological analysis of the frustrations, the pent-up emotions, and the tensions which provoked the outbreak, the story was too long for *The Crisis* and we had regretfully to suggest that it be offered elsewhere. In May, 1945, however, we carried her study in affection, "Olaf and his Girl Friend." And in November we published "Like a Winding Sheet."

Mrs. Petry thus joins that company of brilliant young writers, Langston Hughes, et al., who first received publication in the pages of *The Crisis*.

After one of the Mifflin editors had read "On Saturday the Siren Sounds at Noon," he asked Mrs. Petry if she were working on a novel. She was[1] and the

---

1. In James Ivey's interview we are told that Petry answered Houghton's query by saying that she was writing a novel. In the article "Street Wise," which appeared in *The Hartford Courant* on November 8, 1992, Garret Condon reports that Petry responded to Houghton's query by saying she was *not* working on a novel but might be shortly. The Chronology, which was edited by Ann Petry, indicated that in 1944 Houghton first asked Petry about writing a novel. At that time she replied that at the time she was not but would eventually. Petry also says that the editor who approached her was female, while Ivey writes that the editor was a man.

following year she submitted the first five chapters and a complete synopsis of *The Street*. She was then awarded the $2,400 Houghton Mifflin Literary Fellowship for 1945. This enabled her to devote the next ten months to finishing the novel.

The Street was published in January and its appearance gave me an opportunity to meet Mrs. Petry. My appointment was for 11:30 A.M. in the offices of Richard Condon in East 57th Street, just off Fifth Avenue. Mrs. Petry met me cordially and was eager to record that her first published story in *The Crisis* had given her [her] reputation.

In person Mrs. Petry is of medium height, [with] pleasant manners and intercourse, and possessed of a sense of companionable good humor. She has a creamy-brown complexion; alert, smiling eyes; and a soft cultivated voice. We entered at once into the intimacy of talk and the first thing I wanted to know was how she had come to write her first published story.

"Did you have any particular message in that story? What were you trying to show?" I queried.

"Nothing in particular. I wrote it simply as a story. But it came to be written in this way. One Saturday I was standing on the 125th Street platform of the IRT subway when a siren suddenly went off. The screaming blast seemed to vibrate inside people. For the siren seemed to be just above the station. I immediately noticed the reactions of the people on the platform. They were interesting, especially the frantic knitting of a woman on a nearby bench.

"I began wondering," continued Mrs. Petry, "how this unearthly howl would affect a criminal, a man hunted by the police. That was the first incident. The second was a tragedy I covered for my paper. There was a fire in Harlem in which two children had been burnt to death. Their parents were at work and the children were alone. I imagined their reactions when they returned home that night. I knew also that many Harlem parents, like Lilly Belle in the story, often left their children home alone while at work. Imaginatively combined the two incidents gave me my story."

I then asked her where she got her knowledge of the West Indian background for "Olaf and his Girl Friend." Many of her friends and acquaintances, she explained, are West Indians, and they often tell her stories about the islands and discuss West Indian customs.

"I wrote that story to show that there can be true affection among Negroes. That Negroes can love as deeply as anyone else. So many people impute to Negroes an unhampered sensuality that I felt it time to tell the truth. Now the idea of Olaf's [the chief character in the story] seeking Belle Rose through the sailor's grapevine, I got from a friend."

"What writers have influenced you?" I asked.

"Really," replied Mrs. Petry, smiling, "I have read so many authors and so many books that I don't know. I have been an omnivorous reader since childhood. I was born and reared in a small town, and in a small town, you know, there is really nothing much to do except read."

I then asked her about her recently published novel, *The Street*.

"In *The Street* my aim is to show how simply and easily the environment can change the course of a person's life. For this purpose I have made Lindy [*sic*] Johnson an intelligent, ambitious, attractive woman with a fair degree of education. She lives in the squalor of 116th Street, but she retains her self-respect and fights to bring up her little son decently.

"I try to show why the Negro has a high crime rate, a high death rate, and little or no chance of keeping his family unit intact in large northern cities. There are no statistics in the book though they are present in the background, not as columns of figures but in terms of what life is like for people who live in over-crowded tenements.

"I tried to write a story that moves swiftly so that it would hold the attention of people who might ordinarily shy away from a so-called problem novel. And I hope that I have created characters who are real, believable, alive. For I am of the opinion that most Americans regard Negroes as types—not quite human—who fit into a special category and I wanted to show them as people with the same capacity for love and hate, for tears and laughter, and the same instincts for survival possessed by all men."

Mrs. Ann Petry was born in Old Saybrook, Connecticut, and comes from a New England family that has specialized in some branch of chemistry for three generations. Her grandfather was a chemist; her father, an aunt, and an uncle are druggists. Mrs. Petry is herself a registered pharmacist, a graduate of the college of pharmacy of the University of Connecticut. It was while working as a registered pharmacists [*sic*] in the drugstores owned by her family in Old Saybrook and Old Lyme that she began writing her first short stories.

If she had not married and gone to New York City to live, she would undoubtedly have continued her career as a pharmacist. Instead she sought and found jobs in New York that would give her an opportunity to write. She sold advertising space and wrote advertising copy for a Harlem weekly. She also edited the woman's page for a rival weekly, and covered general news stories.

While interviewing celebrities, covering political rallies and three-alarm fires, and reporting on murders and all other forms of sudden death, she acquired an intimate and disturbing knowledge of Harlem and its ancient evil, housing; its tragic broken families; its high death rate.

She spent nine months working on an experiment in education that was being conducted in one of the city's elementary schools and thus observed at firsthand the toll that segregated areas like Harlem exact in the twisting and warping of children's lives.

In addition to working on newspapers she has taught salesmanship, written children's plays, acted with an amateur theatrical group. She is a former member of the now famous American Negro Theatre. She has studied painting, and plays the piano for her own amusement, claiming to be the least promising pupil of a well-known composer and pianist. At present she is executive secretary of Negro Women Incorporated, a civic-minded organization which keeps a watchful eye on local and national legislation.

From Interviews with Black Writers
John O'Brien

Mrs. Petry is presently working on another novel, after taking several years off to raise a family and write children's stories. We met in early November of 1971. She picked me up at the train station in Old Saybrooke [*sic*] and, on the way to her home, showed me the landmarks that dated back to before the Revolution. She was quick to point out disdainfully the ugly encroachments of commercialism upon her town. She lives in a house that was built in 1800 and has been preserved in its original state. Because she dislikes tape recorders, as well as interviews, she answered my questions by mail a few months after we talked in her home. Almost a year after our initial meeting, we talked briefly once more on the phone in an effort to expand on some of her earlier remarks. The brevity of her answers and her obvious hesitancy to talk about her work belie her warmth. After apologizing for what she considered to be unhelpful answers, she invited me to visit her again when I was not armed with pen and paper.

INTERVIEWER: Do you like talking about your writing?

PETRY: No. I find it painful.

INTERVIEWER: Is it just that it's unpleasant for you, or do you think a writer shouldn't discuss her own work?

PETRY: I personally don't like talking about it. My feeling is that once I've written something I don't have anything more to say about it. That's it. Talking about it isn't going to change what I did or didn't do. The classic example of the man who tried to explain his work was Shaw. Well, it seems to me that if you have to explain what you write, then you haven't done a very good job. If a critic wants to analyze it, let him. Fine. But I don't want to.

INTERVIEWER: Are you also hesitant to talk about the craft of writing?

PETRY: No, I don't mind. But I'm not an authority. I can only speak in terms of what I try to do or the problems I face.

INTERVIEWER: Do you have any particular difficulty in creating characters?

PETRY: I don't have any particular problem in creating characters. They seem to grow and develop and become alive during the process of writing. Occasionally there's something about a character I don't know. For example I had almost finished writing *The Street* and I still did not know why Mrs. Hedges always wore a turban. One afternoon I was on the Eighth Avenue subway going to the Bronx and it suddenly came to me that Mrs. Hedges was bald. And then I worked out how she came to be bald.

INTERVIEWER: Do you have a set way in which you begin working on a character? Do you know beforehand what he or she will be doing in the story?

PETRY: There are really so many ways. I don't think that a character appears in its entirety. It's part of a process whereby you have probably surprised yourself several times by the time you have finished, because the character changes or grows or does things that you did not expect. It comes to you as you write.

INTERVIEWER: Then you never start out by thinking of a character as having to fulfill some symbolic function in the story?

PETRY: No, because I do not think of characters functioning symbolically. I hope that what starts out as a sketch will become a full-boned portrait, but that portrait is not necessarily very much related to the original sketch.

INTERVIEWER: Then the creation of a character, for you, is instinctive?

PETRY: Yes. I don't think that I can explain the origins of a character, or even why he fits the situation he's in.

INTERVIEWER: There's a complex system of imagery in your short story "In Darkness and Confusion." I wonder whether you were conscious of it as you wrote?

PETRY: I don't think I worked it in consciously. It's something that I became aware of after I finished it. That particular story almost wrote itself. I did it all at one sitting. I don't know about other people, but it seems to me that the subconscious mind is what creates such things in a story.

INTERVIEWER: Do you ever become aware that something is taking on symbolic importance while you are writing a story?

PETRY: I guess that it's always a matter of after the fact, but I always shy away from such things as symbol hunting. If they are there, they are not there because I consciously created them.

INTERVIEWER: How much do you depend upon personal experience for material in your stories? Must you experience, in some way, much of what you write about?

PETRY: I think a writer would be seriously handicapped—well, let's say limited—both as to subject-matter and the creation of characters if these were based solely on personal experience.

INTERVIEWER: I know that you worked as a reporter in Harlem for six years. Did this experience affect your writing in any way, perhaps both your style and subject matter?

PETRY: Doubtful.

INTERVIEWER: When we met at your home last November we talked about critics' frequent arbitrary grouping of black writers which is most apparent in anthologies of black literature. So often critics seem to ignore the differences between black writers in order to establish some mysterious link between them all.

PETRY: That's because we're all black. As I said, we do have a common theme. We write about relationships between whites and blacks because it's in the very air we breathe. We can't escape it. But we write about it in a thousand different ways and from a thousand different points of view.

INTERVIEWER: Does it bother you that, as John A. Williams has complained, regardless of what a black writer does in his work or what subject he may treat, he or she is always designated as "a black writer"?

PETRY: Well, it's just an indication of the fact that black people are in a minority in this country. If I lived in a country where the majority of the people were black people I would be an "author"—and the white folks would be "white authors"—if they were authors.

INTERVIEWER: I wonder whether such identification does not force a black writer always to direct himself only to black audiences? Do you find yourself writing with a particular audience in mind?

PETRY: Not at all. If I permitted myself to think in terms of the reader, I would become so inhibited I wouldn't write—at least for publication.

INTERVIEWER: In addition to the racial problems black writers face in America, they also share the problem that all American writers have—our culture does not greatly value books and reading. What do you identify with the culture you write in?

PETRY: Pro-football, beer, TV serials, and cars.

INTERVIEWER: Have you ever been unable to write a story which you would have liked to write?

PETRY: I've never abandoned a story or a novel once I started working on it. I've abandoned many ideas before I ever put a pen to paper. I once planned or thought about writing a book for young people about Daniel Drayton and Edward Syres, two ships' captains imprisoned for attempting to help slaves escape from the District of Columbia on the schooner *Pearl*. I didn't write that particular book because I became interested in—actually fascinated by—a slave, Tituba, who was one of three women charged with witchcraft at the beginning of the trials for witchcraft in Salem, Massachusetts. Another idea that I once abandoned was to write a book for young people about Jacintha de Siquiera "the celebrated African woman—founding mother of the richest of all Provinces of Brazil" [David Davidson]. I gave up this idea because of the research involved—I would have had to spend a considerable amount of time in Brazil, and I would have had to learn to speak Portuguese, or at least learn to read it. These ideas go with the territory and I hope someone else will write about these people. Feel free.

INTERVIEWER: Is there a part of a novel which is more difficult for you to write than any other?

PETRY: Sometimes. I had great difficulty writing the chapter [*The Narrows*] in which Link is murdered.

INTERVIEWER: Is there some point in the novel where you feel that you have everything in hand and the rest will fall into place?

PETRY: I never have a novel "in hand" until it is completed.

INTERVIEWER: Do you ever experience any conflict between meaning and form, or between what you might like to do in a novel and what you think your reader will be able to understand? Or does the form of a novel develop on its own?

PETRY: The form finds itself.

INTERVIEWER: Do you remember how old you were when you first started to write?

PETRY: Fourteen.

INTERVIEWER: Were you anxious to show your work to people?

PETRY: I rarely ever told anyone that I was writing. And I still don't talk about what I write if I can avoid it.

74

INTERVIEWER: Do you think of your fiction as autobiographical?

PETRY: I could say that none of my work is autobiographical, or that all of it is—everything I write is filtered through my mind, consciously or unconsciously. The end product contains everything I know, have experienced, thought about, dreamed about, talked about, lived for. And so in that sense I am any of the characters that I create, all of them, some of them, or none of them.

INTERVIEWER: Could you say something about your writing habits? When do you work? How much revising do you do? Are you subject to moods during the time you are working on a novel?

PETRY: When I'm writing I work in the morning from 8:00 A.M. to about noon. If I'm going to do any revising I do it in the afternoon. The first draft is in longhand. The planning and the writing go hand in hand for the most part. I revise endlessly. And yet the first chapter of *The Street* was written in one sitting and that first draft was the final one—no changes. And there were no changes in a story entitled "Like a Winding Sheet" or in "Sole [*sic*] on the Drums." I do not work at night if I can avoid it. I am not subject to moods. I doubt if my family or anyone else can tell when I'm thinking about writing.

INTERVIEWER: One reviewer of *The Street* made a comparison between you and Theodore Dreiser. Do you see any similarity? Do you feel that you belong to a naturalistic school of writing?

PETRY: No to both questions. To be absolutely honest about it, it really doesn't interest me. I always want to do something different from what I have done before; I don't want to repeat myself. If I belong to a certain tradition, I don't want to belong, because my writing would be very boring if I always wrote in a particular style.

INTERVIEWER: Could you tell me how the conception for *The Street* came to you? After you have an idea for a novel, how do you go about starting the novel itself?

PETRY: *The Street* was built around a story in a newspaper—a small item occupying perhaps an inch of space. It concerned the superintendent of an apartment house in Harlem who taught an eight-year-old boy to steal letters from mail boxes. As far as procedure is concerned I usually make a rough outline or draft—and I break it down into chapters, and begin to write, and then revise what I've written.

INTERVIEWER: Hoyt Fuller noted in an article that a number of black writers around 1950 abandoned writing novels about blacks. He pointed to *Country Place* as an example. Why do you think this happened with so many black writers? Why did you choose different subjects and themes?

PETRY: I don't know what impelled other black writers to stop writing novels about blacks. I wrote *Country Place* because I happened to have been in a small town in Connecticut during a hurricane—I decided to write about that violent, devastating storm and its effect on the town and the people who lived there.

INTERVIEWER: A few critics have pointed out what they think are your implausible endings, especially those in *The Street* and *Country Place*. I guess what they are referring to are Lutie Johnson's act of murder and Lil's attempted murder. How do you respond to that criticism?

PETRY: I don't think there's anything "implausible" about the endings in *The Street* and *Country Place*—they're perfectly logical given the circumstances and the character of the people.

INTERVIEWER: Why did you use the druggist to narrate *Country Place* rather than having an omniscient point of view as you did in *The Street*?

PETRY: I had never used the first person, and a druggist in a small town seemed to offer great possibilities.

INTERVIEWER: One of your critics has argued that the hope of the town in *Country Place* resides in the minority figures, Neola and Portegee. One also might add the youth, Johnnie Roane. Did you intend something like this? And at the end of the novel there appears to be a restoration of moral order when several minority figures are included in the will. Were you suggesting that social and moral change must occur simultaneously?

PETRY: No to both questions. I think you're reading something into this book that simply is not there.

INTERVIEWER: What are your feelings about Weasel? His name suggests certain unlikable qualities, yet, in some crude way he brings justice to the town, even though he does not always practice it himself.

PETRY: As to The Weasel—very few people are all evil. The Weasel isn't, Mrs. Hedges isn't, nor is Powther in *The Narrows* or Bill Hod. We're all mixtures of good and evil.

INTERVIEWER: So Mrs. Hedges in *The Street* plays a kind of dual role: she rescues Lutie and Bub on two different occasions, yet she was also part of the vicious system that was entrapping them.

PETRY: Dual role? Well, perhaps. Mrs. Hedges is probably a classic example of the fact that most people are a mixture of good and evil.

INTERVIEWER: *The Narrows* seems a very different novel from the first two. Perhaps your form and content have come together perfectly in that novel. What do you think?

PETRY: I don't know.

INTERVIEWER: Is there any "correct" point of view in *The Narrows*? I think of this in relation to the themes of guilt and time. Abbie thinks that the past determines everything and that she, personally, is responsible for the evil that has occurred. Miss Doris thinks that everyone is responsible. Bill Hod and Weak Knees think of racism as being the cause of the evil. Is any one of these wholly correct?

PETRY: I suppose not, though racism comes closer to being *the* cause.

INTERVIEWER: Is there any implicit condemnation of Link for having undertaken the love affair with a rich white girl?

PETRY: No.

INTERVIEWER: Could you say something about the use of comedy in *The Narrows*? Some of the comic scenes seem to be steeped in "black humor."

PETRY: I have a peculiar sense of humor.

INTERVIEWER: While I was reading *The Narrows* I was struck by certain thematic similarities to Huxley and Faulkner, especially in your treatment of time. Are you conscious of any such resemblance?

PETRY: No.

INTERVIEWER: The racial conflict in *The Narrows* is minimized. Although it plays a large part in determining the outcome of the story, you seem to be treating more universal problems. Do you think that "race" is as important a theme in this novel as it was in *The Street*?

PETRY: Yes.

INTERVIEWER: Your short story "The Witness" ends with Woodruff slowing his car after he is reminded what the boys had done to him. Will he return and be a witness against them? Of is it just that he doesn't have the strength or desire to go on?

PETRY: He won't be back.

INTERVIEWER: What are your plans for writing?

PETRY: I plan to go on writing novels and short stories and one of these days I plan to write a play—or two—or three.

INTERVIEWER: Did you intend "Mother Africa" to be an allegory? For example, the protagonist is called "Man." Or is it unfair to ask you to explain your own story in this way?

PETRY: I think it is an imposition to ask me to "explain" a story or a novel.

A Visit With Ann Petry, May 16, 1984
College of Pharmacy, University of Illinois at Chicago[2]

ROBERT MRTEK: Let me tell you again how grateful we are to have you here. The group that you're with now is a small class of pharmacy students, everywhere from first year students to fifth year students (fourth year professional students), and they are all taking a course called "Images of Pharmacy in the Arts." We are in the section of the course now when we are looking at writers who have either a very close association with pharmacy themselves, or who write extensively about pharmacy in their literary creations. And, we are particularly fortunate, again, to have you here because you are both a pharmacist and a very famous writer.

    As you know, I am making a tape of this and you will have the right to edit the transcript; the students have agreed that they will sign off their rights "in perpetuity" and we intend, with your permission, to deposit this in the Archival Division of the American Institute of the History of Pharmacy.

---

2. Robert Mrtek, professor of pharmacy administration, and Suzanne Poirer, professor of pharmacy education, team-teach the course "Images of Pharmacy in the Arts" at the University of Illinois. They invited Ann Petry, a pharmacist turned writer, to visit and to talk about, among other things, pharmacies as settings in several of her writings.

Let me tell you that the period will be as freewheeling as you and the students are to make it. They have all read "Miss Muriel" and that chapter that we saw dramatized out of *Country Place*.

CONLIN [student]: And "The New Mirror."

MRTEK: Thank you.

PETRY: Now, if you will ask questions, I'll do my very best to answer them.

MRTEK: I think that would be fine.

PETRY: It's, I'm sure, pretty obvious that "Miss Muriel" and "The New Mirror" and another short story of mine called "Has Anybody Seen Miss Dora Dean?" are all related in one way or another to the drugstore that I talk about and write about. The question is always asked, "How much of this really happened? Did you experience this?" Well, yes, some of it did, some of it didn't. In "Miss Muriel," there was only one person who had a real existence as far as—no, two people: one was my uncle (I think I refer to him as "Uncle Johno") and the other one is the man who arrives every summer as a guest of Uncle Johno. Now the man who arrived every summer really existed. He had been a teacher of English. He had been an actor. Usually the first thing he said to me on his arrival was, "These Yankees have destroyed your voice."

MRTEK: What did he expect?

PETRY: He said, "You're talking through your nose." But he was endlessly entertaining and really a great person to be around.

My aunt really did exist: she was a druggist. She graduated from the Brooklyn College of Pharmacy in 1908. She was the only woman in her class. I have her diploma and that is really fascinating because every single professor that she had signed it. There are flowers depicted in the name "Brooklyn College of Pharmacy," The "B" is all decorated with flowers, and the "C's" and so on and so on. When I showed it to my daughter she said to me, with considerable puzzlement, "What have flowers got to do with pharmacy?" I said, "Well, you forget that this is a very, very old profession. It has not always been called pharmacy, but originally, almost all the things used in the treatment of illnesses came from flowers, from roots, from herbs. These days they may be made chemically, but originally they came from plants—from the leaves, the seeds, etc."

As I said, my aunt really did exist. Of course, her name was not "Sophronia," but she did exist. She was very beautiful, and we did have in the town a little old man who was a shoemaker, who developed this sort of, very frightening, attachment to her. Nobody actually ran him out of town, that's all made up. He did finally marry somebody else. But before he married he came with this little bag of trinkets that had belonged to his mother. He gave these to her because he said he knew this wasn't going to work out. She was a very young woman, but then on the other hand she never did marry. And as for the piano player, he never existed but she did have a suitor that my family regarded as highly unsuitable, but that was it. Yes?

LOWRIE [student]: Were you also the only woman who graduated from your pharmacy class?

PETRY: Oh, no, there were five of us.

MRTEK: But you were the only black woman.

PETRY: Yes. My father and a friend were the first black men licensed as pharmacists in the state of Connecticut back in 1890. I still have his license. Of course, in the days when he became a pharmacist, he was apprenticed in a drugstore because there were no pharmacy schools.

MRTEK: In American pharmacy history, we find examples, particularly in the South, where pharmacy practitioners and blacks were separated by law; Negroes were not permitted to handle or manipulate any drug substances because of the racial discrimination. Now, let me ask you, in your father's time—in your own time—was that black discrimination very much there in practice? In other words, being a black pharmacist, were you set on earth to prepare pharmaceuticals for black people only?

PETRY: No.

MRTEK: That never materialized within the community?

PETRY: No, not at all. As a matter of fact as far as the community was concerned, if we had had to depend on black people for a living, we wouldn't have survived because there weren't any, except for one other family, and that was it. But, no, when my father first opened his drugstore in the town, someone who was very much like the Weasel in *Country Place* did arrive to tell him—brought him a message saying that "they" were going to run him out of town. And my father, who was a man of uncertain temper and not given to receiving such messages, promptly took him by the throat and almost choked him to death and said, "You go back and you tell *them* that any time they want to try, I walk on this street around nine o'clock at night. And tell them to try"—and he said—"You be sure to tell them that I come from Madagascar." And he always said that he didn't have any idea where Madagascar was or what it was. But he said he figured they'd be so frightened by the idea of confronting a man from some unknown part of the world that no one would bother him. And they didn't.

Their customers were white, all of them. If they had any feelings about us they concealed them. There was only one doctor. He served the town I lived in and five or six other towns. Quite often he was not available no matter what the emergency might be—he could be miles away. People brought anyone who had been injured to our drugstore. My father would do his best to patch them up until the doctor arrived. Oftentimes it was a matter of saving someone's life.

And when he died the whole town, well, practically the whole town, turned out, filling the church with mourners, spilling out to the sidewalks— young, old, middle-aged.

MRTEK: He was "Doc."

PETRY: Yes. Except that my father was black. "Doc" of *Country* was white.

BROSSART [student]: Was it that family influence that made you choose to go into pharmacy?

PETRY: Oh, of course, I'm sure. My family did not say, "You must study pharmacy" or anything like that when I finished high school. I was very young—only 15, and my sister who was older than I was, was already going to a fancy Ivy League college, so finally they said to me, "Why don't you try to go to pharmacy school?" So I said "Sure. When?"

BROSSART: You mentioned that there was one other black family in the town that you lived in. Do you think that they might have held something against your family, that they wouldn't have anything to do with you? Do you think it might have been because of your association and professional relationship with all the white people in town?

PETRY: That hadn't developed. We had just barely moved in. We were really very [laughs] very presentable.

SUZANNE POIRER: You mentioned—your narrator in "New Mirror" expresses some annoyance at times with being the daughter of the pharmacist, feeling "We're on display in the town, why do we have to act and behave certain ways both because we're the pharmacist's family and we're one of only two black families?" Did you yourself ever feel that your life had some inequities inasmuch as—some unfairness because—you were the pharmacist's family, and your home and business were in the same building?

PETRY: Well, home and business, true, they were in the same building, but there was a very definite demarcation—my family had really literally built a wall between the society, that is the village and the people in the village, and the drugstore. The drugstore was a public thing, but our family life was not. And I would imagine that to this very day that people in that village really don't know very much about us. At all. And, as far as I was concerned, I suppose I was like any other lively youngster. I found that wall not exactly acceptable.

Let me tell you something else I still think of often. I told you that I had an aunt who was a pharmacist. And I can remember my mother saying to me and my sister and a cousin of mine that never under any circumstances in public were we ever to call her "Aunt Louise." She was always to be "Miss James," because otherwise this whole town would call her "Aunt Louise." They would prefer to call her that rather than call her "Miss James." And to this day, do you know, I refer to her as "Miss James." She lived to be ninety—ninety-four, I think.

MRTEK: When did your interest in literature and in writing first awaken and how did it—if you can remember that?

PETRY: Well, I was writing so to speak while in high school. I had an English teacher, Miss Avery. It was a small high school and the English class was up at the top of the building, which was literally like an attic. In those old buildings you can smell the oil they used to oil the floor with to keep the dust down, and it was powdery with chalk.

I used to get very bored. Miss Avery and I didn't like each other at all. Anyway, we were reading *A Tale of Two Cities* and because I had this terrible habit—if I really got into it I'd read the whole book. You're supposed to read a chapter every day. Then when I came to class, you see, I could spoil it for everybody.

Well, anyway, I think it was the final exam in English—we were sophomores and Miss Avery had given us what we regarded as an awful question. She did not ask us specifically about the characters, or the plot, or the author or anything that we might think she would ask. Instead she said we were to write an imaginary scene between any of the characters—it didn't make any difference which ones—and you can well imagine that any young people in any English class absolutely would have died. Well, anyway, I thought, an imaginary scene . . . . You remember Jerry Cruncher, the gravedigger? I wrote the most marvelous imaginary scene. I mean, I just sat there and enjoyed myself—making it up.

A few days later, Miss Avery arrived in class with all these papers. She looked around the room and said, "I want to read you one of these papers." She read my paper, and I thought, "She's doing this because she's going to say 'This is a terrible example of what people can produce if they don't pay attention in class.' " But she didn't say that at all. She said she thought it was wonderful. And after class she gave me back my paper and she said to me, "You know," with this note of wonder in her voice, "I think if you really wanted to you could write."

I think Miss Avery had such a hard time with that English class; she later became a missionary, and she went to India.

BROSSART: Did everybody else pass?

PETRY: No, a lot of them didn't. But you asked me when I became interested in literature. I developed a love for poetry when I was in high school. We had an English teacher who, if we had a few spare moments, would read a poem to us. One day he read Robert Frost's "I, Too, Am a Swinger of Birches." Birch trees are so limber that if you would swing on them, you could swing a long distance. This is about a boy who discovers birch trees, and I was simply enchanted. I became a reader of poetry afterwards. And I was trying to think . . . .

MRTEK: Do you have a favorite poet?

PETRY: Indeed I do. But I have something I wanted to read to you.

MRTEK [to the group]: That was the journal that she keeps. You see, she told us in the room downstairs to keep a journal . . . .

PETRY: Yes, but this I think is so absolutely amazing. It suggests what a long way we've come. When we finally closed that drugstore I found a great many old bottles. One of the boxes I found in the cellar contained a patent medicine. It was called "Kennedy's Medical Discovery," and it sold for a dollar and a half. Now you have to remember that in the days when they were selling patent medicines like that the average worker in a rural community earned about three hundred dollars a year, so that a dollar and a half for a bottle of medicine was a really large amount of money.

And this particular patent medicine is described as "the greatest medical discovery of the age—Kennedy's Medical Discovery. Mr. Kennedy of Roxbury, Massachusetts, discovered in one of our common pastures a weed." It's a remedy that cures "every kind of humour from the worst scrofula down to a common pimple." He has tried it in over eleven hundred cases, never failed—except in two cases—both thunder puma [?]. He has now in his possession "over two hundred certificats [*sic*] of its value—all within 20 miles of Boston. Manufactured by Donald Kennedy." And there's a picture of him with his mutton chop whiskers and his hair is rather long. It also says "Entered according to act of Congress in the year 1854 by Donald Kennedy in the Clerk's Office at District Court in Massachusetts." And embossed on the side, "Kennedy's Medical Discovery," and then it says also "Dr. Kennedy" embossed but it doesn't say that on the label.

This is what it says on the label: "Two bottles are warranted to cure a nursing sore mouth. One to three bottles will cure the worst kind of pimples on the face. One to three bottles will clean the system of biles. Warranted to cure the worst kind of humour in the mouth and stomach." And then he goes on to the eyes, the hair, "ulcers, corruption to the skin, ringworm, rheumatism, salt wounds, scrofula." And also, if your lungs are infected with "shooting pains" it will take care of that. It'll take care of any kind of "biliousness" and on and on and on.

MRTEK: Sounds like *Tono-bungay*—which we have read in this class.

PETRY: But isn't that amazing, and it is a very handsome bottle, greenish in color.

MRTEK: Tell us something about the techniques of writing. How do you go about producing the works that you do? Are they all outlined first? Do you cogitate on them or do you just freewheel with the typewriter?

PETRY: On, no, I don't freewheel it. But in the case of *The Street*, for example, I'd written an outline—no, not an outline, a synopsis of the first five chapters. The short stories, only because I usually like to know where and how the thing's going to end. If I have an ending in view it's easier to work directly toward that. With books that I've written for children, I'm usually much more careful about organizing . . . .

MRTEK: Why is that?

PETRY: Because I feel that children's books ought to have a kind of, that they should have about them something that makes you feel that they're—I guess you'd say an inevitability—that I don't think you could achieve by just shooting off. And then of course, you rewrite. And you rewrite and you rewrite.

MRTEK: We have in this class all struggled with writing this quarter and I'm glad to hear you say you rewrite, because we rewrite and throw away.

PETRY: That's right.

MRTEK: Do you throw away?

PETRY: Absolutely.

MRTEK: It doesn't come out perfect?

PETRY: It never has. In fact, I can even tell you the instances where something I wrote remained exactly the way it was when I started. The first chapter in *The Street* I wrote last. I don't think I changed anything, but that's the only thing that I can think of where that's true, because all the rest of that book I wrote and rewrote and . . . .

MRTEK: So many writers talk about writing as possessing them. Hemingway describes it that way. It couldn't be forced, or it couldn't be encouraged. It just sort of descended on the writer and then the writer had to grapple with it. Are you pretty even in your ability to write or does it . . . .

PETRY: Well, I suppose all . . . . I must say this, though: he may have said all that, about it descending on him, but I'm sure, from the way his—the things he wrote—it's perfectly obvious to me that he wrote and rewrote, because otherwise he couldn't have achieved that clean, clear kind of prose. I don't think that just comes like that.

POIRIER: Earlier, this noon, when you were talking about the characters in *Country Place*, you said that "Doc" was partly your father but your father was not as even-tempered. How can that be—the influence of the real characters on created ones? Some writers talk about creating a character and then the character kind of creates him- or herself and leads the writer. Does that happen?

PETRY: Yes, of course. It does. Of course whenever that happens, I think it's wonderful because I think you get a much more believable character.

POIRIER: Do you usually start with a picture of someone or something in mind and then just kind of let it grow?

PETRY: Well, now, let me think. I—I suppose I do, I don't know. I was trying to think of the short stories that . . . . I do remember that I always intended to use that business about bats in the drugstore because that did actually happen. And I just thought it was so wonderful because all of a sudden on a hot summer's night these bats were floating around in the drugstore, creating a considerable amount of consternation. And I always thought that somehow I had to put that in a story.

LEWIS [student]: Eyes are very important in the works that I know about you, and I was wondering if somehow your characterizations some way began with the eyes. I was thinking about your minute description of bats and eyes. And then eyes—I don't remember all the eyes, but I just remember that eyes are very dominant. They almost could be a motif. You see the eyes and you know the character.

PETRY: Don't you think that's true of people?

LEWIS: Well, that's what I was wondering: if you are a very keen observer of one's eyes.

PETRY: Well, I try to be an observer of everything about people, but eyes are particularly important.

MONTELLA [student]: In "Miss Muriel" it seemed that the little girl—it just reminded me—maybe you were writing part of yourself into that character. Do you ever do that in your stories: Do you write yourself into your stories?

PETRY: Well, I think, actually, I'm in all of them. I'm even part of the Weasel. Really. I think that we all have—let's see—how am I going to say it? I think we're all sufficiently complicated as people to be able to . . . it's a matter of putting yourself in somebody else's place. And because there is in me, or in you, well, certain qualities which may not be dominant ones or the ones that show on the surface, they are there somewhere.

CONLIN: Apart from your literary work, do you ever regret leaving pharmacy and going into writing, and was there any point in your life after you have left pharmacy that you wanted to go back into that profession?

PETRY: Well, no. I never have regretted it, but the reason probably, I'm quite certain, is that I worked for my family in the afternoon when I was in high school. I worked seven days a week. The only time that drugstore was closed was on Christmas in the afternoon and Thanksgiving in the afternoon. And that's the reason—long hours and very little pay—made me pro-labor and pro-union. And once I was out of it I had no desire to return. It's true that I'm sure that if it had been a different kind of situation other than that . . . as a matter of fact, if it weren't for that experience I would probably have tried to become licensed as a pharmacist when I lived in New York City.

BROSSART: Did they pay you the going rates?

PETRY: No.

MRTEK: Oh, maybe that's the reason.

PETRY: It was that, and the hours. I mean who on earth would ever consent to working seven days a week? Good heavens, that's terrible. I'm sure you won't have to work more than thirty-five or forty hours a week. Look at all the time you have to do other things—reading, writing.

TAM [student]: Did you enjoy it when you were in pharmacy school?

PETRY: Yes, I did.

MRTEK: I want to go back to something you said about your preparation for the children's stories. You talked about the quality of inevitability. Beethoven was often described as trying to achieve that same quality of inevitability in that [*sic*] music. The risk of inevitability is that spontaneity goes out the window.

PETRY: Not if it's a good story. Not if it's good music.

MRTEK: How do you keep the magic and variety and yet make everything exactly "inevitable"?

PETRY: Well, I don't think that's difficult. I think if you have a kind of enthusiasm for the subject matter: for example, the more I learned about Harriet Tubman, the more I learned about Tituba of Salem Village, the more involved I became in the lives of these women, and the more I admired (and incidentally, you know, when you talk about the healing arts, I think both those women practiced them: Tituba in Salem, which is one of the ways that she got into difficulty, and Harriet Tubman, who looked after so many people when she was on those trips North. I mean there was a nurturing quality that they had. And I think that people in what I call the healing arts, if they're really good, they have it). And if you write about people like that you don't have any problem. You get caught up in their lives, in their motivation.

The only problem that I have in writing these books is that I really and truly don't like going back in time where you have to check every single thing in terms of clothing, in terms of food, in terms of the way the houses look inside. All of that—it slows you down. But other than that . . . and you know, that's really kind of amazing, because those books, by now I don't know how many years old they are, and they still sell. They are still in print.

And one of the most rewarding things about writing books for children, for young people: all year long while school is in session, all of a sudden your mail will come and there's a whole stack of letters. Yes, and it's just . . . from children who have read what you've written, and they have questions and they express their appreciation.

LOWRIE: Tell me more about the lack of distinction between pharmacy and medicine back in that era. I had a grandfather who was a small-town doctor in Graff, Ohio, and the house was attached to his office. I used to go visit him all the time. You know, I grew up in Chicago, so to me, that was the sticks. We used to go visit him, and he had this one part of his office where he would sit and make drugs.

PETRY: Sure, he was dispensing then.

LOWRIE: Yes, and then I didn't think anybody ever went to a pharmacy after seeing him, so back then there really wasn't a line of distinction at all.

PETRY: No, I'm sure there wasn't. Of course, I don't know how far back you're talking about, but originally, no.

LOWRIE: Well, the earliest I remember is late 50s, early 60s.

PETRY: Oh, there was beginning to be a distinction then because by that time there was a, I would say, gentlemen's agreement: the pharmacists did not practice medicine and doctors did not dispense.

LOWRIE: Even in small towns?

PETRY: Even in small towns. And the only reason my father was—oh, he wouldn't have said he was practicing medicine—but the only reason he was doing what he did was because there were no doctors available, so what could he do—let one bleed to death on the floor in his store? But in the early days I would say the distinction between medicine and pharmacy was nonexistent.

MRTEK: In the old days, medicine had three branches to it. One was physic, the art of diagnosis, the second one was surgery, and the third was pharmacy. They were all part of the same thing.

I wanted to ask you what your feelings are on today's attitudes toward a visual society. We have—young people claim today that they relate much more directly to an image—pictorial image—than the spoken work. And for some young people it is very difficult to even experience your art.

PETRY: I'm sure it is. But I have no—you can't do away with television; it's out of the question. The only thing that really bothers me: it would seem to me, it would be increasingly difficult, for example, to handle all the material that people have to handle in these professional schools. They have to do a tremendous amount of reading and studying and if you're not geared toward the printed word, well, I think you would have problems.

I remember one thing that bothered me and I've thought about it ever since, and that's some time ago: when Kennedy was president, he said that television is the greatest psychic destroyer in the world. And I often thought about that and what it comes down to, I guess, is that people no longer relish or welcome being alone; they no longer, if you want to use the word meditate: they don't do that. They have to have some kind of image before them, some kind of noise or sound in their ears and that is a destroyer of the self.

MRTEK: It robs us of our imagination.

BROSSART: That's why I'm having such a hard time on this paper. [laughter from class]

PETRY: Could I ask some questions? I'm very curious—how do you feel about what I said? Is that true, do you feel that television, or that watching it, has in any way diminished your response to the printed word?

BROSSART: Well, I know from my experiences, when I read a book compared to when I see a movie, I get a lot more out of my reading because I can put my imaginary images onto people and how they're going to look and everything. After I've read a book and I go and see the movie, I feel it wasn't as deep as it was, you know; the response isn't as deep as when I was reading the book. I think you can ad lib your own feeling, your own emotions and everything in the reading, but when you see it on the screen, it's all there and you can only accept it for what it's showing there. I think there's a big difference there, in interpretation.

PETRY: Do you write?

BROSSART: I think about it.

MRTEK: But one cannot write without thinking.

How about some of the others of you?—We spent almost a full quarter agonizing over readings, plays, art work . . . .

CONLIN: I think that the visual medium takes a lot away. The movie is going to happen in an hour and a half, and if you're going to get everything out of that movie you have to get it all out of it in that span of time. Whereas, when you're reading you can stop and think about things and maybe read part of it today, and think about it, pick it back up tomorrow and continue with it and just go at your own pace, and you can get a lot more out of it than if you have to be able to get everything out of something in a set period of time. And I think that's one way that the visual medium takes it away from you.

BROSSART: Being a student, though, I think we don't really watch T.V. as much as your average . . . .

PETRY: How true!

BROSSART: It's true, when you work and you go to school and you study, you know you're lucky if you might catch the evening news. I mean, that's how it is for me and a lot of my friends.

POIRER: You were saying in one of the conversations we had before you came, that you had gone back to your writing to find references to pharmacy and things that were in there that you hadn't noticed . . . .

PETRY: Oh, I didn't find—I didn't really have the time to do that. But here and there a little—this afternoon for instance, I've mentioned *The Street* where a man had been cut and goes to the druggist, and I mentioned the fact that Tituba of Salem Village and Harriet Tubman were healers in the best sense of the word, and of course, *Country Place*. And the short stories that I have written where I used the drugstore as a background and the pharmacist appears in the pharmacy. There is also my children's book *The Drugstore Cat*. There is something though that . . . . I wrote a book for children called *Legends of the Saints*, and I looked and one segment in there has to do with St. Martin de Porres. He was a barber originally but he was also a person who dispensed medicine. He was a practitioner of the healing art. And that's—I suppose it's that really, and I guess that all came from pharmacy.

CONLIN: Have you ever written about pharmacy?

PETRY: You mean as such?

CONLIN: Yes, as a profession or a story about pharmacy?

PETRY: Well, yes, a long time ago. I wrote—there was a publication called *Drug Topics* (is it?)—Well, a good many years ago I wrote a piece I called "A Tribute to Mr. Gentry." Mr. Gentry was a purely imaginary pharmacist, and I wrote about drugstores and the way they once were and the role they played in small communities and, in fact, in the large ones. Yes?

MONTELLA: What are your feelings about today's pharmacists?

PETRY: Today's pharmacists?

MONTELLA: Yes.

PETRY: Well, I mean, I don't know that I have any particular feeling, I have great respect for them professionally and I certainly think that they are far better educated and equipped to handle all the chemicals used in a very complicated world. I say complicated world as far as business is concerned.

MONTELLA: It's a lot faster-paced and productive . . . than how it was in the past?

PETRY: And, of course, I think pretty much all that life of the small-town drugstore—I think that has vanished. I think that even today, for example, you don't see the pharmacist. It would never occur to you to go in a back room and talk to him.

MRTEK: Weasel would never have had the opportunity today that he had.

PETRY: No.

MRTEK: He would have to know how to read a computer screen.
       What is the Ann Petry style? How do you describe yourself?

PETRY: My lifestyle?

MRTEK: No, no, not your lifestyle—unless you care to talk about it?

PETRY: Well, I live in a small town in an old, old house that was built in 1790. We shore it up here and there once in awhile. And to my daughter's disgust every time (of course, she doesn't live at home any more; she is married and lives in Philadelphia) . . . but anyway, when she was growing up if I wasn't around to answer the telephone, I'd be way off somewhere and somebody wanted me, I'd say, "Tell 'em I'm mowing the back forty." But anyway, we have gardens and grow flowers and vegetables. And I read a lot, I write a lot.

MRTEK: But in terms of literary style . . . .

PETRY: All I ever try to do is to write so that the reader will keep on reading. And I try to write so that what I've written will be remembered, whether it's a character or a situation or believable dialogue that will leave a lasting impression.

LOWRIE: Is your husband a writer also?

PETRY: Well, yes, in a way. He used to write copy for an advertising agency. He is now retired. I used to tour and give lectures. I spent a year at the University of Hawaii, and naturally when you write you become an object of great curiosity. One of the first questions that people used to ask me was, "What does your husband do?" And I would look them right in the eye and say, "If I were a man, would you ask me what my *wife* did?" How near are we to closing because I've got something I want to read.

MRTEK: Please read.

PETRY: I'll read it right now. But first I urge you to write in a journal—almost every day, and to write short stories. Maybe write poetry. But write. You have to offset the life of chemistry and biology and all of the science that you study during these years in this school of pharmacy by developing another side of your mind and of yourselves. So I leave you with these lovely words written by Laurie Lee, a British poet: "Any bits of warm life preserved by the pen are trophies snatched from the dark, are branches of leaves fished out of the flood, are tiny arrests of mortality." You are quite young, and probably not the least bit interested in immortality, but someday you will be. Keep dreaming. Keep writing. Keep reading. Enjoy.

MRTEK: Thank you very much.

A MELUS *Interview: Ann Petry—The New England Connection*
Mark K. Wilson

The interview took place in midsummer of 1987 in Old Saybrook, located on Long Island Sound at the mouth of the Connecticut River and aptly described by Petry as "a picture-postcard of a town." We talked in the comfortable dining room of the house where Petry and her husband, George, have lived for the past forty years, scarcely half a mile from the town green and the drugstore once owned by Petry's father when, in 1908, she was born in the second-floor family quarters. Petry speaks of her present house, built around 1790, as having "great vibes," and certainly her warm hospitality puts the visitor immediately at ease. Despite her professed discomfort with interviews in general and tape recorders in particular, she agreed to let me place a recorder on the table between us as we talked for several hours about her life and work. But no transcript can really convey the warmth of her responses, often punctuated by laughter, or the relaxed and gracious atmosphere of her home.

INTERVIEWER: Your stories are full of storytellers. There's Dottle Smith in "Miss Muriel"; in *The Narrows* there's Malcolm Powther, who, for all his primness, is a wonderful storyteller; and there's Miss Doris, who holds J. C.

and the eavesdropping Abbie spellbound with the story of Mr. Orwell. You must have known storytellers as you were growing up.

PETRY: I did, yes. The first ones were right there in my own family. My father was a great storyteller, and he loved to tell stories about his family. And they were absolutely incredible stories. And sometimes I've used them in— well, in *The Narrows*, for example.

INTERVIEWER: Are they the stories of the Major's family in that novel?

PETRY: Yes, that's right. My mother's stories were not nearly as colorful or as interesting. They had to do with a household and the happenings within it. But, then, my mother had these brothers; I often make reference to them and to the stories that they used to tell. One of them had an enormous farm in Weathersfield, just outside Hartford, but the other uncles were footloose and fancy free. They never married. They had literally lived all over the world. They had been stevedores, pullman [sic] porters, barbers. And they were storytellers, and their stories were just plain wonderful. One of them, Uncle Bill, had been in the Spanish American War, and he had all kinds of stories. I grew up with these stories, and I've told them over and over again in various ways.

INTERVIEWER: You mentioned using them in *The Narrows*; are some of them also in the stories of the Layen family, the Wheeling stories?

PETRY: That's right, in those short stories. Yes, definitely.

INTERVIEWER: Those stories seem to draw heavily on your own life experience as well as on the family stories you grew up with.

PETRY: They do, in many ways.

INTERVIEWER: Your maiden name was Lane, and the narrator's family name is Layen. Your father, like the narrator, was the druggist in a small New England coastal town; and both the Lanes and the Layens lived in the same building as their pharmacy, the only black families in their communities.

PETRY: Right, absolutely. Of course, I ought to tell you one of the things my mother said to me. After I started writing she said, "Please don't write about this family!" [laughs] But I did. I don't think she knew it; I don't really think she did.

INTERVIEWER: Your narrator in "Has Anybody Seen Miss Dora Dean?" remembers how as a child she created a fantasy scenario for the mysterious suicide of Mr. Forbes, and even narrated it to an imaginary audience. Did you ever do that kind of thing as a child?

PETRY: Absolutely, yes. You see, this town where I grew up was a very, very small community; and we had to entertain and amuse ourselves. Of course, naturally, we read; that was free, and available. And also here was this family of storytellers, and so it was just inevitable that as a kid I would make up stories about people.

INTERVIEWER: Do you remember particular things you read as a child?

PETRY: My mother used to read aloud to us. But I can very well remember the first book that I read all by myself, and that was *Little Women*: I think I was in the second or third grade. And all of a sudden I understood why it was people sat and read books even when it was beginning to get dark and they were still sitting there reading; that was wonderful! And then of course after that I read everything I could get my hands on.

INTERVIEWER: Do you remember what you especially liked about *Little Women*?

PETRY: Well, I do remember Jo, who was a tomboy, was a person who I could—I could understand her. For instance, there was a place in there somewhere she said that sometimes when the air was cold and the wind was blowing she could just breathe and breathe and breathe it, and it made her feel like she could run forever. I can understand that.

INTERVIEWER: And of course Jo was going to become a writer, too.

PETRY: Yes! She was, yes.

INTERVIEWER: Did you have the sense, even as a child or adolescent, that you wanted to become a writer?

PETRY: No, not really.

INTERVIEWER: Do you remember when you realized that that was what you wanted to do?

PETRY: Well, I think that it started actually when I was in high school. We read *A Tale of Two Cities*, and we had an English teacher—we weren't particularly fond of each other—and she gave us this test in which there was only one question: you were supposed to write an imaginary scene from that book. And I sat down and wrote this scene between Jerry Cruncher, who was the gravedigger, and his wife; I don't even remember what it was, but it was one of the few times that, when I was young, all of a sudden I just wrote and wrote, and it didn't make any difference whether it made sense or not— I just wrote it. And when we went back, Miss Avery, the teacher, said: "Now, I've got something I want to read to you." And I sat and listened in horror, because she was reading aloud what I had written and, of course, I thought she was going to say: "This is an example of what you should never, ever do!" But instead she said that I had written it; and she said, "You know, I honestly believe that if you wanted to, you could become a writer." It never had occurred to me that I could be a writer; and even then I don't know that I ever said to myself at that particular stage that, yes, I wanted to become a writer.

INTERVIEWER: In fact, you went on to study pharmacy. Was that the result of family encouragement?

PETRY: No, there was never any pressure. I just decided that I was going to study pharmacy, and of course my family was very pleased.

INTERVIEWER: You've mentioned *Little Women* and *A Tale of Two Cities,* Alcott and Dickens. Do you remember other writers you enjoyed?

PETRY: Oh, when I was quite young, of course, I went through all the children's classics—you know, *Little Lord Fauntleroy, Black Beauty,* those books. And then gradually went on: I read Dickens and went on from that, particularly in fiction.

INTERVIEWER: Were there American writers in your high school courses that you remember reading?

PETRY: Yes, Poe, some of the short stories. Let's see. Oh yes, and Hawthorne. And of course poetry, a lot.

INTERVIEWER: You once mentioned Thoreau as a writer you admire, a New England writer who was important to you. Do you remember at what point you read him?

PETRY: Well, I must have been in my early twenties. I'd never felt comfortable with a lot of "things"; I don't know whether that's the right way to put it or not, but clothes and things like that just never made a very strong appeal to me. I think my mother gave me the first copy of *Walden* I ever had, and I was so impressed by it—to think that anybody would go and lead that kind of simple, uncomplicated life. And it did have a tremendous influence on me.

INTERVIEWER: Are there any black writers that you remember reading either in high school or in your own early years as a writer?

PETRY: There were two in particular: *Narrative of the Life of Frederick Douglass* and James Weldon Johnson's *Autobiography of an Ex-Colored Man.*

INTERVIEWER: Are there writers that you return to, that you go back and re-read?

PETRY: Well, let's see. I read, or re-read, Faulkner. And Malamud is one of my favorite writers, especially some of his short stories, which I think are great—also a novel of his called *The Fixer*, which is very moving.

INTERVIEWER: Your third novel, *The Narrows*, is dedicated to Mabel Louise Robinson. Could you tell me who she is or was and why you dedicated the novel to her?

PETRY: Mabel Louise Robinson was a professor of English at Columbia. George was in the Army; I was working for the *People's Voice* and trying to write short stories, and I was just getting back rejection slips. I decided that there must be some better way than that, and I read a book by Arthur Train called *My Day in Court.* This was his autobiography, fascinating, and in it he said: "If I wanted to be a writer and I was young, the first thing that I would do would be to go to Columbia and see if I could enroll in Mabel Louise Robinson's workshop course in writing." And I thought, "I wonder if it still exists?" So I got hold of a catalogue, and it did, and it said to get in you had to submit a story and have an interview. So I made an appointment for an inverview and took in my story in my hot little hand.

INTERVIEWER: Do you remember what the story was?

PETRY: Let me see. . . . No, but in any event I had the story. I can see her now: she looked me over very carefully, and she sat and read the story in front of me, which is also embarrassing. Then she put it down and looked at me and said, "Well, that's a very good story." I thanked her, and she told me when the course met, and that was it. Well it was really and truly quite wonderful. There were only five people in that class, and they were all females; all the men had gone off to war. And so we literally did have her undivided attention. We were supposed to submit a story every three weeks. We had to read each other's stuff and talk about it. And she was really, I think, about as wonderful as it would have been possible for anybody to be. She was truly interested in us, truly committed to our becoming writers.

INTERVIEWER: Do you remember any specific things that you may have learned from her?

PETRY: Well, one of the things she used to say to us over and over again—let me see, how did she put that? "Truth is a —truth is a millstone around the neck of a writer." People would write things and she'd say, "You can't do it this way." And they'd say, "Well, it's true." She would say, "You cannot use that exactly as it was. Sometimes maybe, but most of the time no. You have to make it dramatic."

INTERVIEWER: That makes me more curious about your own use of "truth" as she described it—actual events from your own life that may figure in your fiction. Obviously every writer does it.

PETRY: Yes, but you don't just use these things; they have to be worked into and a part of the whole. They can't just be stuck in like raisins or plums or something. They have to be mixed in.

INTERVIEWER: Can you think of specific instances, of events in your own life or outside events that you have incorporated into your fiction in this way, that you've made use of by transforming them into part of the whole?

PETRY: Well, in that story that you mentioned, "Has Anybody Seen Miss Dora Dean?," actually there *was* a man who did commit suicide, and my family did conjecture about it—about what happened, what caused it. So here was something that was, I hope, transformed into a believable story.

INTERVIEWER: In the stories, several times I would be reading and I would wonder—

PETRY: "Did this really happen?"

INTERVIEWER: For example, in "Doby's Gone" Sue Johnson is a first-grader and she is taunted by her white classmates and called a "nigger," and she fights back and is victorious. Did you as a child in an all-white community have a similar experience?

PETRY: Well, yes indeed. My sister and I went—you see, my sister's two years older than I am, and of course there were no kindergartens in Saybrook then. And when she was going to start first grade, I said I had to go too. And my mother said, "You can't; you're too young." Because I was only four. And my father said, "Oh, let her go; they'll just send her home." But they didn't. Anyway, here we are, all decked out in our new clothes with our hair in braids and everything. And we went to school, and everything was just fine. But then when we came back home, they stoned us! Can you imagine?

INTERVIEWER: The other school children?

PETRY: Yes, they threw stones at us, and we arrived home crying, covered with bruises and cuts, and our ribbons were gone. And we said, "We don't want to go back to school!" My mother said, "Yes, you'll go back to school; it will be all right." And she took us back the next day. And when we start home and get to a certain place, all of a sudden these boys start throwing stones at us; and suddenly two of my uncles appear. And they knock the boys' heads together and threaten them with dire consequences: murder, mayhem, arson. Under no circumstances were they ever to come near those little girls again!

INTERVIEWER: And there were no repercussions?

PETRY: No.

INTERVIEWER: That sort of family solidarity is a strong element in your stories. The Layen family seems both a part of the Wheeling community and yet a separate community unto itself. Did you and your family experience that sort of double existence?

PETRY: Yes, we did. The drugstore was the public place of our lives. My parents never let it intrude on their private lives. They created a whole separate world. I always thought all families did that: I know we did. And there was always a cause for celebration: either it was somebody's birthday, or it was an anniversary, or there was *something*. There was always a great gathering. And you would not know the rest of the town existed except that we were always happy to see people and cordial and invited them to tea or something. My father sang in the church choir. He helped raise the money to build this town hall. He and three other men used to sing stuff from Gilbert and Sullivan all over the county. In other words, he was part of the community, and yet not part of it. He had a big family, warm and close-knit, and my mother did too. So we always had people from both sides of this family who were around, telling their stories and so forth. There was always this separate private world that had nothing to do with the town.

INTERVIEWER: Were there ever intruders into that world, like Mr. Bemish in "Miss Muriel"?

PETRY: Occasionally.

INTERVIEWER: Was there a real Mr. Bemish?

PETRY: Yes, there was a Mr. Bemish.

INTERVIEWER: And was he in fact run out of town?

PETRY: Well, let's say he left [laughs].

INTERVIEWER: The young Layen daughter who tells the story in "Miss Muriel" can't decide whether she objects to Mr. Bemish as a suitor for her aunt because he's white or because he's old. And then she adds something very interesting: "I do not know exactly how I've been 'trained' on the subject of race." And you put "trained" in quotation marks. Why the quotation marks?

PETRY: Because I suppose that's not a word you would use in terms of educating a young person. I mean you don't train them in terms of race. And *she* did that; I mean, those are her quotes. She herself knew that this wasn't done that way. Somehow she didn't know how she had arrived at the conclusion. She didn't really know whether she objected to him because he was white or because he was old, but actually I don't think she objected to him because he was white. I think it was more because he was old.

INTERVIEWER: Getting back to Mabel Louise Robinson and her advice to transform "true" events by making them dramatic, do you recall other suggestions she made?

PETRY: Well, she told us to read plays and go to the theatre, because she said, "Here's an art, and it takes great skill to tell a story only in terms of dialogue." And she said all people who write fiction would benefit from the knowledge that they could get from reading plays and going to the theatre.

INTERVIEWER: I read somewhere that you yourself had been connected with—

PETRY: The American Negro Theatre? Yes, I was.

INTERVIEWER: And did you perform with them?

PETRY: Yes, I did, for about a year or two. It was great fun. I used to play there at the 135th Street Library. Downstairs they had the equivalent of a small theatre, and we had a play that was written by Abe Hill called *On Striver's Row*. We put it on three nights a week. And there were a lot of famous people who had their start, you know, in that theatre.

INTERVIEWER: Do you remember who some of them were?

PETRY: Oh, sure. Ruby Dee and Ossie Davis. Harry Belafonte. Let's see . . . there was Helen Martin. And Fred O'Neal, Sidney Poitier, and Hilda Sims.

INTERVIEWER: Many of your stories seem to me not only dramatic but even cinematic. The novels, particularly, seem almost made for the screen. Have you had nibbles for filming any of them?

PETRY: Oh, yes. Nibbles, and there once was an outright sale, but I guess they got terribly cold feet. I don't even remember which one of those outfits . . . .

INTERVIEWER: What was the novel?

PETRY: *The Narrows*. And then I guess they decided that this was not something that they thought they could get away with, so to speak, because here was this love affair between this black man and a white woman. So nothing ever came of it.

INTERVIEWER: When would that have been?

PETRY: Oh, good heavens: around 1955, something like that.

INTERVIEWER: Speaking of *The Narrows*, you said to John O'Brien that you had trouble with the chapter in which Link gets killed. Do you recall why that was?

PETRY: Well, because it seemed to me that here was this man who in so many ways had to battle to survive; and he *had* survived—and had survived, I would think, fairly whole as a person. And that the end of his life should have been like that—I had trouble with that.

INTERVIEWER: It was painful to write?

PETRY: Yes, really. Because, you see—as he grew up you always had this memory of this little boy who was truly abandoned by a woman who is intelligent and kindly, really, at heart; but nevertheless she doesn't even remember that he exists because she is so completely devastated by her husband's death and because she feels guilty about it. So that when it came to this young man who, I think, was great. . . . But on the other hand, the instant that he had said to these people, "We were in love," it was a death sentence; and there was no way, logically, that he would not be killed.

INTERVIEWER: You've told how you were strongly encouraged by Mabel Louise Robinson. Did you receive similar encouragement from other writers?

PETRY: I didn't know any writers, no.

INTERVIEWER: For example, Arna Bontemps reviewed both *The Street* and *The Narrows*. And you had no personal contact with him at the time?

PETRY: No, I didn't meet him until—oh, it was a long time after that. Somebody was making recordings of people who had written stuff for children, and Arna Bontemps was one of the people who were down at the place where we recorded. That was the first time I met him.

INTERVIEWER: How about Richard Wright, whose *Native Son* and *Black Boy* had gained him wide recognition by the time you published *The Street* in 1946. Did you have any contact with him?

PETRY: No, I had no contact with Richard Wright, though I read his novels and short stories as they were published. And I also read the work of Langston Hughes, James Baldwin, and Ralph Ellison—with admiration for all of them, including Wright. *Invisible Man* is a truly great novel.

INTERVIEWER: In *Country Place*, Johnny Roane feels that he has to get out of Lennox, his country place, in order to do what he wants to do. At the end of the novel he's going to New York to study painting. Did you feel that you had to get out of your "country place" in order to do what you wanted to do?

PETRY: Do you mean get out of Saybrook?

INTERVIEWER: Yes.

PETRY: No, I don't know that I did, really. The only reason I left was because I married George Petry and he lived in New York. So I went to New York to live, but I don't know that I ever thought that Saybrook was a place I had to leave.

INTERVIEWER: Do you think your writing career would have developed in the same way if you had stayed in Old Saybrook?

PETRY: I doubt it. After all, the kind of experience I had in New York in terms of work I never could have had here in Saybrook. In the first place, in New York I worked for newspapers in various capacities. And I certainly never would have been in Mabel Robinson's class; I wouldn't have been a member of the American Negro Theatre. I assume all of these things were undoubtedly helpful to me in my writing.

INTERVIEWER: What led you to come back to Old Saybrook? Was it just the end of the war?

PETRY: Well, I had suddenly become famous in a way which I think it would be very difficult to describe, and I *hated* it! I mean, I just didn't feel that this . . . I couldn't, I couldn't cope with it. I mean, I just didn't . . . I didn't *want* people asking me questions; I didn't *want* people interviewing me; I didn't *want* to have somebody always taking my picture. I decided there must be another way to live. So I left.

INTERVIEWER: And did you find what you wanted?

PETRY: Yes, I did.

INTERVIEWER: The New England town you came back to, Old Saybrook, seems very like the town of Lennox in *Country Place*, and yet it's not a very favorable picture that you paint of Lennox in that novel. Johnny Roane remembers things he disliked, in particular, "the town's smugness, its satisfaction with itself, its sly poking fun at others." I was wondering about how the novel was received in Old Saybrook in 1947. Did the townspeople recognize themselves and take offense?

PETRY: I don't think it ever occurred to them that that was Old Saybrook. I don't know.

INTERVIEWER: Have you ever had reaction from New Englanders to your portrayal of New England characters?

PETRY: No, not that I know of.

INTERVIEWER: I wanted to ask something about your relationship to New England. In his review of *The Narrows*, Arna Bontemps refers to it as "a New England novel." And Sybil Weir has recently written about that novel as a New England novel. Yet you said in a paper you read last year at the University of Massachusetts in Amherst that you do not see yourself as a New Englander. I wonder if you could comment on that.

PETRY: Well, when you consider my background, true, I guess for maybe three or four generations my family, one side or another, has lived in New England. But I think in that paper I started off by saying that if your ancestors came from England, Scotland, Wales, whatever, the chances are that when they were little somebody dandled the baby on their knees and sang "Ride a Cockhorse to Banbury Cross." But my grandfather James (that was on my mother's side) was a runaway slave from a plantation in Virginia; and so when he sang to his children, dandling them on his knee, it was: "Run little baby, run; paterollers goin' to come!" "Pateroller" was the word that slaves used for "patrols"; they never said "patrols." All right, so that's part of my background; that does not a New Englander make. In other words, this is another breed entirely. And though we take on all of the—what shall I say?—the speech patterns, we accept the kind of food, the cooking, the houses, and so forth, nevertheless truly we're not New Englanders—and never will be, as far as I can see. When you stop and think, for instance, that here we were, these little girls going to school, and were *stoned*! Why? Because we're the wrong color, in the wrong place, at the wrong time. And when my sister, for example, was accepted at Pembroke—you know, which is part of Brown University—and my mother took her over there to Providence with all her new clothes and things: she gets there in the registrar's office and there's great goings and comings, and rustling and whispering, and so forth. And they say she'll have to wait. And finally comes from the dean's office the dean of women and says, "Well I'm so sorry, but your daughter cannot stay in the dormitories. Black girls cannot stay in the dormitories. There's a fine nice family at such-and-such a street, and that's where those girls would have to stay." My mother of course goes and calls my father and says, "What do we do now?" "Well," he said, "you're there.

Go look at the place; see what kind of family it is. If they seem to be good, decent people, she stays." So she stayed. Well, that does not a New Englander make!

INTERVIEWER: What does make a New Englander?

PETRY: You have to be, I would assume, born here for generations, and nobody ever stoned you, nobody ever told you you couldn't stay in a dormitory, nobody. . . . When my father opened his store, for example, they told him they were going to run him out of town because they did not want a black druggist in this town. That does not a New Englander make.

INTERVIEWER: Do you see a distinction between that sort of "outsiderness" and that of, say, a Hester Prynne and little Pearl, who also had stones flung at them in *The Scarlet Letter*?

PETRY: Yes, that's true.

INTERVIEWER: The racial element of course makes it different. Are you saying simply that you will never be an insider?

PETRY: No, not in my lifetime. Maybe in somebody else's lifetime.

INTERVIEWER: When you were in the Connecticut College of Pharmacy, were there any other blacks in your class?

PETRY: No, there weren't any. And when my aunt, Miss James, graduated from the Brooklyn College of Pharmacy in 1908, she was the only woman in the whole class, and the only black as well. And that was a long time ago. I often think what an extraordinary person she was. And we've all survived and flourished, but I still have this feeling that we're not really New Englanders.

INTERVIEWER: And would you like to be a New Englander?

PETRY: Well, I'm quite happy with the way I am, thank you. [laughs]

INTERVIEWER: I ask partly because it seems to me that many of the black characters in your fiction tend to fall into one of two broad and contrasting categories: the prim or the primitive. I realize I'm oversimplifying.

PETRY: Yes, I understand what you mean.

INTERVIEWER: On the other hand there are the Abbie Crunches who do seem to want to be New Englanders and, in fact, *are* very New England.

PETRY: Absolutely, absolutely, totally, yes.

INTERVIEWER: Malcolm Powther thinks of Abbie: "She had New England aristocrat written—"

PETRY: ". . . all over her."

INTERVIEWER: And then there's Malcolm Powther himself, and there are others in your fiction. Even Diana the kindergarten teacher in your most recent story, "The Moses Project." And Mary Lou Brown, Turner's wife in "Mother Africa."

PETRY: That's right, yes. But then there's Mamie Powther! [laughs]

INTERVIEWER: Exactly. Abbie Crunch and Mamie Powther. These two seem to epitomize the two poles I was talking about. What accounts for the difference between these two types?

PETRY: Well, you can't account for them; these are people who are the way they are. Any society has all kinds of people in it, and this one does too.

97

INTERVIEWER: What makes it particularly interesting is the dynamics of the interaction between these two kinds of black people—because Abbie Crunch, of course, is offended by Mamie Powther.

PETRY: Yes, her very appearance offends her [laughs]. It just happens that these people are so interesting if you take and put them together—and particularly if you take a Mrs. Crunch and put her under the same roof as Mamie Powther.

INTERVIEWER: In a way Emmanuel Turner in "Mother Africa" combines both kinds of blacks that we've been talking about: he's "Junkman, Ragman, Old Man Turner, 'Man' Turner" in his junkman phase; and then he undergoes a kind a metamorphosis—

PETRY: Right.

INTERVIEWER: —and gets his first shave in twenty-five years, or something like that.

PETRY: [laughs] And I love the fact that the barber says he knew that someday something like that would happen.

INTERVIEWER: Do you know whether Turner is going to revert to his more primitive "junkman" self?

PETRY: Oh, I think he'll revert; I think he will!

An Interview with Ann Petry
from Artspectrum *(Windham Regional Arts Council)*

Ms. Petry's work contains a remarkable range of subjects and sentiments. She writes sometimes with a sense of outrage, sometimes with exuberance. She frequently writes of white injustice toward blacks but never descends to stereotyping; she views all her characters objectively. One of her most compelling characters is Mrs. Gramby in *Country Place*, an elderly white woman. Her narrators range from an eleven-year-old black girl to a middle-aged white man. Her protagonists are young and old, white and black. Throughout her writings, Ms. Petry challenges prejudice, pettiness, and injustice at all levels of our society. She has been one of the central forces in the twentieth century demanding a reevaluation of existing stereotypes, particularly of blacks and of women, and urging the destruction of existing boundaries between individuals and between social groups. Ms. Petry is currently at work on a novel.

Following is an interview with Ann Petry.

Q. It must have been a great change moving from Old Saybrook to New York City after you were married.

A. Well, I had visited New York fairly often, so it wasn't a total culture shock. The part of it that was truly shocking to me was when I saw the poverty in Harlem. That was not like any poverty I had ever heard of. We lived in Harlem for quite a while. I worked for a weekly publication based in

Harlem, *The Amsterdam News*. Then we moved to the Bronx. My husband was drafted and went into the army, and I lived by myself. It was at that time that I decided I would become a writer or I wouldn't. So I decided I would give myself a year in which to do it. The only kind of jobs I had were part-time jobs that didn't involve any total commitments of my time. We had a friend who was an artist in an advertising agency and was working on a catalogue for wigs. He called me and asked me if I'd do the writing, so I said, "Sure, why not?" And it brought me quite a nice sum of money. So I lived on the wig money for a long, long time. Every time I see someone wearing a wig, I feel very grateful.

Q. And this is the time you wrote *The Street*?

A. Yes.

Q. After *The Street* you wrote *Country Place*, which represents quite a change of subject matter since it describes life in a small New England town, where all but one minor character are white. What made you decide to write such a different novel?

A. I was in Old Saybrook during the hurricane of 1938. It was a frightening experience; I never forgot it. I thought that I ought to use that storm in a novel, and why not place it in Old Saybrook, where I experienced it? And of course Old Saybrook is mostly white, so the novel has mostly white characters in it. Besides, I have never wanted to write the same kind of book twice. Writing such a different book was a challenge, but one that I welcomed.

Q. Then came *The Narrows*. That, too, was favorably reviewed, but I understand some readers objected to the relationship between Link and Camillo [*sic*].

A. If you really want to stir the flame of prejudice, then you confront someone with a black man and a white woman. The other way around nobody really gives a hoot. The book sold a lot of copies, and the critics were kind. But everyone questioned the relationship between these two people. And I don't find anything unusual about it. Men have fallen in love with pretty faces, have had passionate attachments to women who were not their intellectual equals—there's nothing unusual about that. Personally, I think that it's a darn good story.

Q. Sometime in the late '40s, you started writing children's books. Why did you decide to do that?

A. With my parents, all my aunts and uncles, and my sister and me, we were a very old family. Then my sister, who was two years older than I, had a child. And I felt I had to do something to welcome it into this old family. So I wrote *The Drugstore Cat*. Then after that—I don't remember now exactly how or why I happened to look at some American history textbooks that were being used in the schools. I read the sections that had to do with slavery, and I was appalled. I thought, "Now, look at all these youngsters growing up in this country, whose only knowledge, really and truly, of black people is what they read in these books." The blacks were always portrayed as happy in slavery. They could all sing and dance. They were immoral, for the most part. And I thought, "Well, there has to be somewhere along the line books that portray slaves in a different way. And a good place to start is books for children." Then quite by chance, I was up in Hartford, and met a man there who asked if I had ever thought about writing a book about Harriet Tubman. I said I didn't even know who Harriet Tubman was. So I began looking up stuff about her, became fascinated, and wrote a book about her. After that I decided to write a book about the Witchcraft Trials. I did some reading on them and became very interested in Tituba, a young slave woman who was one of the women accused of and imprisoned for witchcraft, and decided to write about her. And also, incidentally and along the way, I learned more about witchcraft than people should ever know. I became fascinated, and collected all the materials I could.

Q. Most books about the Salem Witch Trials logically explain away all elements of witchcraft. But in your work, Tituba is actually depicted as having supernatural powers.

A. I did not set out to argue that witchcraft does not exist. It happens all over the world. I have had relatives with conjuring powers. The point I was making about Tituba was that she had not done anything wrong. She had not bewitched anyone; she was a good and decent person.

Q. You come from a tradition of strong and unconventional women. As you explain in your autobiographical essay, your mother and aunts were businesswomen, financially independent, who refused to be traditional housewives.

A. They were certainly not traditional women in any sense of the word. I have often marvelled at how good my parents' marriage was, considering how unusual my mother was. But they loved each other very much. Perhaps my father thought all women were like that.

Q. Your novels contain many very strong women, few strong men.

A. Well, that's the way of the world.

Q. Do you consider yourself a feminist?

A. I don't like labels like that. I'm just an individual who has a special way of looking at the world. But I am an ally of feminists, there's absolutely no question about that.

Q. How has your view of the world changed over the years?

A. I don't think my views have changed much. If anything, I see the world as getting worse. As far as race relations go, worse things happen in New York now, and even right here in Connecticut. The attacks on people, that I find terrible, absolutely terrible. And I don't even remember attacks like that a few years ago. I don't know what has changed. It's frightening.

Q. So you don't think the Civil Rights Movement has changed things very much?

A. I think it did, but then I don't know what happened. On colleges campuses, for instance—why is there all this conflict between white students and black students? And when you read the statistics about life in Harlem—things haven't changed there.

Q. Your daughter is an attorney. You don't feel that her generation has an easier time of it than yours?

A. No, definitely not. I guess it's the same world.

Just a Few Questions More, Mrs. Petry
Hazel Arnett Ervin

In her hotel room in Philadelphia on the morning of February 4, 1989, some hours before she was to appear as the guest of honor at the Fifth Annual Black Writers' Conference, Ann Petry agreed to meet with me for an interview. Several months after our talk, she answered follow-up questions by mail. In this interview, there are no particular themes. As the title suggests, my purpose is merely to ask additional questions—questions that have arisen from previous interviews and from rereadings of her novels by other critics.

Q. In *Black Women Writers at Work*, Maya Angelou names you as a writer who has impressd her. She says she would walk fifty blocks in high heels for something you've written. And according to Ms. Angelou, for a country girl, that means a lot. How do you feel about her tribute to you?

A. Oh, what a beautiful statement! I had no idea.

Q. You are best known for *The Street*. It is your most written about work. Is there another work for which you would prefer to be remembered?

A. I'd like to be remembered for everything I've written.

Q. We have so many superb black American women writers, but are there novelists who have impressed you?

A. Women?—particularly Toni Morrison and Alice Walker.

Q. And males?

A. Ralph Ellison's *Invisible Man* is truly great. And Langston Hughes. I have enormous admiration for Langston Hughes.

Q. When did you first discover Langston Hughes?

A. I discovered Langston Hughes's poetry while I was living in Harlem—thought it was great.

Q. What about another popular person associated with Harlem—Zora Neale Hurston?

A. I read *Their Eyes Were Watching God* about five years ago.

Q. Shortly after you moved to New York City in 1938, you enrolled, first, in a writing workshop, then, in a class in which Mabel Louise Robinson was your teacher. How helpful was Robinson in shaping your writing style and technique?

A. Mabel Louise Robinson did not shape my style or technique. She did something more important than that: she taught me how to criticize my own work, and other people's work. Perhaps even more importantly, she made me believe in my own ability.

Q. So, what you're saying is that your writing career began with your learning to believe in your own ability? How, then, did you find your own voice?

A. I acquired skill in the art of writing fiction, and nonfiction, by studying, analyzing, [and] dissecting novels, short stories, plays, [and] biographies created by other writers, and by rewriting my own work.

Q. Upon writing and publishing your first short story, "Marie of the Cabin Club," you used the pen name Arnold Petri. Why a pseudonym? Was it because you were then a would-be writer? Or a woman? Or . . .

A. Neither. I am a "private person." I did not want my friends, acquaintances, and colleagues to know that I was writing short stories.

Q. The story has one of the most favorable portrayals of a black man: Georgie Barr is a gentleman, well-traveled, successful, articulate, handsome, heroic, and something of an 007-adventurous type. There isn't a blemish. I realize I have made a comment here, but will you comment?

A. No comment is necessary.

Q. Well, is there a conscious effort after this story to portray a less romantic and a more representational black male?

A. No.

Q. Yet you never again duplicate or romanticize about the black male.

A. That's because I have no interest in writing a series of novels and/or short stories involving characters I've [already] created.

Q. But how do you develop characters and plot? Where are the influences?

A. I develop the characters in my books to the point where I could probably give a lengthy report on their likes and dislikes—including what they ate for breakfast on any given morning—their hopes and their fears, their peculiarities, what they do for a living, etc.

Q. And your plots?

A. . . . from items in newspapers, from the weather, from conversations, from gossip, etc. For example, in recent years, I've been intrigued by newspaper stories about "house arrest." So, I finally wrote a short story about a man who was placed under house arrest: "The Moses Project." From the weather . . . I survived a hurricane in Connecticut. It became the source of a novel: *Country Place*.

Q. May one conclude that you maintain a rapport with your characters?

A. Yes.

Q. Do Lutie and Min from *The Street* and Abbie Crunch and Frances Jackson from *The Narrows* try to set examples for black women who might rely on fictitious black women characters for lessons about life?

A. Their commonality is gender.

Q. In *The Narrows*, Mamie Powther is like a blues lady. Then, there are jazz scenes in *The Street* and jazz scenes in the short stories "Marie of the Cabin Club" and "Solo on the Drums." How were you introduced to jazz?

A. I've been a jazz buff, or a fan, ever since I was a teenager—many a long year ago.

Q. When discussing *The Street*, many critics do not move beyond the question of form. For them, the question remains whether the work is naturalistic and protest or a tragic narrative. What form did you have in mind when you planned and wrote the novel?

A. I did not have a specific form in mind.

Q. Richard Wright mentions in "How Bigger Was Born" that he experienced "mental censorship" when writing *Native Son*, that he worries about what blacks and whites would say about Bigger and whether Bigger would perpetuate stereotypes. How much mental censorship did you experience when you were writing *The Street*?

A. None.

Q. Were there ever concerns on your part or on the part of your editor about *The Street* being overshadowed by or having to measure up to *Native Son*?

A. No.

Q. When *The Narrows* was published, many critics thought the love affair between Link and Camilo was unrealistic. You, however, do not see their love affair as unrealistic?

A. Most people refuse to accept the idea that a black man and a white woman can be in love. "Miscegenation" is a buzzword—causes people to react violently.

Q. In your interview with John O'Brien, you state that you had great difficulty writing the chapter in *The Narrows* in which Link is murdered. I immediately thought of Charles Dickens who cried as he wrote the chapter in *Oliver Twist* in which Nancy is murdered. What made it difficult for you to write about Link's murder?

A. It was like being a witness to the murder of a much loved, much admired friend.

Q. Is the ancestorial link to black culture, so often found in characters in African-American literature, to be found in Weak Knees and Bill Hod in *The Narrows*?

A. Well, maybe. Weak Knees and Bill Hod are trying to give Link a sense of pride in order to survive. What they are using is a survival tactic.

Q. You produced your first three novels during the literary Chicago Renaissance. Was there for you ever a sense of belonging to this movement?

A. No.

Q. Why?

A. I have no idea.

Q. Have you read any of the other Chicago Renaissance writers?

A. I've read all of them.

Q. With all that you have accomplished in your career—work in every genre—I wonder how successful you have been in securing your "own room."

A. Solitude and privacy are essential for a writer. The greatest challenge that remains [for me] is acquiring uninterrupted time in which to write.

Q. What about your actual work habits? I read once that you write from nine to noon, have lunch, and then return and write from one to two-thirty or three in the afternoon; that you write in longhand, type, and then conclude with a final draft. Have such work habits remained consistent throughout your career?

A. Yes.

Index

NOTE: Numbers refer to entries beginning on p. 1.